D0988420

REVISE EDEXCEL GCSE
Physical Education
Unit 1 Theory of PE (5PE01 & 5PE03)

REVISION GUIDE

Series Consultant: Harry Smith

Author: Jan Simister

A note from the publisher

In order to ensure that this resource offers high-quality support for the associated Pearson qualification, it has been through a review process by the awarding body. This process confirms that this resource fully covers the teaching and learning content of the specification or part of a specification at which it is aimed. It also confirms that it demonstrates an appropriate balance between the development of subject skills, knowledge and understanding, in addition to preparation for assessment.

Endorsement does not cover any guidance on assessment activities or processes (e.g. practice questions or advice on how to answer assessment questions), included in the resource nor does it prescribe any particular approach to the teaching or delivery of a related course.

While the publishers have made every attempt to ensure that advice on the qualification and its assessment is accurate, the official specification and associated assessment guidance materials are the only authoritative source of information and should always be referred to for definitive guidance.

Pearson examiners have not contributed to any sections in this resource relevant to examination papers for which they have responsibility.

Examiners will not use endorsed resources as a source of material for any assessment set by Pearson.

Endorsement of a resource does not mean that the resource is required to achieve this Pearson qualification, nor does it mean that it is the only suitable material available to support the qualification, and any resource lists produced by the awarding body shall include this and other appropriate resources.

For the full range of Pearson revision titles across GCSE, AS/A Level and BTEC visit:
www.pearsonschools.co.uk/revise

ALWAYS LEARNING

PEARSON

Contents

This book covers the content for both the full course and short course.

Healthy active lifestyle
1 Health and physical activity
2 Mental benefits of an active lifestyle
3 Mental and physical benefits
4 Fitness benefits of an active lifestyle
5 Health benefits of an active lifestyle
6 Social benefits of an active lifestyle

Influences
7 Key influences: people
8 Key influences: image
9 Key influences: culture
10 Key influences: resources
11 Key influences: health and wellbeing and socio-economic
12 Roles and required qualities
13 Sports participation pyramid 1
14 Sports participation pyramid 2
15 Initiatives and their common purposes
16 Agencies

Exercise & fitness
17 Health, fitness and exercise
18 Health, fitness and exercise and a balanced healthy lifestyle
19 Cardiovascular fitness and muscular endurance
20 Muscular strength, flexibility and body composition
21 Agility, balance and coordination
22 Power, reaction time and speed 1
23 Effects of cardiovascular fitness and muscular endurance
24 Effects of muscular strength, flexibility and body composition
25 Effects of agility, balance and coordination
26 Power, reaction time and speed 2

Physical activity
27 PAR-Q and fitness tests
28 Fitness tests 1
29 Fitness tests 2
30 Fitness tests 3
31 Fitness tests 4
32 Fitness tests 5
33 Principles of training: progressive overload
34 Principles of training: specificity
35 Principles of training: individual differences / rest and recovery
36 Principles of training: FITT principle and reversibility
37 Values of goal setting and SMART targets
38 SMART targets
39 Interval training
40 Continuous training
41 Fartlek training
42 Circuit training
43 Weight training
44 Cross training
45 Exercise session: warm-up
46 Exercise session: main session and cool-down
47 Exercise session: endurance
48 Exercise session: power
49 Heart rates and graphs
50 Setting training target zones

Personal health
51 Requirements of a balanced diet
52 Macronutrients
53 Micronutrients
54 Timing of dietary intake
55 Redistribution of blood flow

Mind & body (Full course)
56 Mesomorphs
57 Ectomorphs and endomorphs
58 Factors affecting optimum weight
59 Anorexia and underweight
60 Overweight, overfat, obese
61 Anabolic steroids
62 Beta blockers
63 Diuretics
64 Narcotic analgesics
65 Stimulants
66 Peptide hormones
67 Recreational drugs
68 Reducing risk through personal readiness
69 Reducing risk through other measures

Cardiovascular system (Full course)
70 Cardiovascular system and exercise
71 Cardiovascular system: adaptations 1
72 Cardiovascular system: adaptations 2
73 Blood pressure and cholesterol

Respiratory system (Full course)
74 Respiratory system and exercise
75 Respiratory system: adaptations

Muscular system (Full course)
76 Antagonistic muscle pairs: biceps and triceps
77 Antagonistic muscle pairs: quadriceps and hamstrings
78 Gluteals, gastrocnemius and deltoid
79 Trapezius, latissimus dorsi, pectorals and abdominals
80 The muscular system and exercise
81 The muscular system: adaptations

Skeletal system (Full course)
82 Functions of the skeletal system
83 What you need to know about joints
84 Range of movement at joints 1
85 Range of movement at joints 2
86 The skeletal system and exercise
87 Potential injuries: fractures
88 Potential injuries: joint injuries
89 Potential injuries: sprains and torn cartilage

Exam skills
90 Exam skills: multiple choice questions
91 Exam skills: short answer questions
92 Exam skills: extended answers 1 (Full course)
93 Exam skills: extended answers 2 (Full course)

94 Glossary
96 Answers
101 Space for your own notes

A small bit of small print
Edexcel publishes Sample Assessment Material and the Specification on its website. This is the official content and this book should be used in conjunction with it. The questions in *Now try this* have been written to help you practise every topic in the book. Remember: the real exam questions may not look like this.

Target grade
Target grade ranges are quoted in this book for some of the questions. Students targeting this grade range should be aiming to get most of the marks available. Students targeting a higher grade should be aiming to get all of the marks available.

1-to-1 page match with the Revision Workbook ISBN 9781446903636

Health and physical activity

You need to know what a healthy active lifestyle is and how to achieve it.

Good health

All aspects of health can be improved through physical activity. Although people of all ages can benefit from physical activity, our REASONS for participating in it may change.

Giving reasons

If asked about the benefits of physical activity, try to give varied reasons. For example, you could give the benefits for different ages: 5, 15 or 50 year olds.

Categories

The benefits of physical activity can be put into three categories:

- PHYSICAL
- MENTAL
- SOCIAL

You need to be able to:

- give examples of the benefits of exercise
- explain how the benefits are achieved
- place the benefits into the correct category.

Some of the benefits of exercise can be placed into more than one category.

If you are asked to justify why you have placed a benefit in a particular category, make sure you give a clear reason.

If you find your choice difficult to justify – check your choice!

Worked example

target G

Which of the following statements describes a <u>physical benefit</u> of exercise? **(1 mark)**

- ☐ **A** Meeting new people
- ☐ **B** Gaining an aesthetic appreciation of movement
- ☐ **C** Feeling better about body shape
- ☒ **D** Losing weight if overweight

EXAM ALERT!

Physical challenge has both **physical and mental benefits**. When you see a question on physical challenge, remember:

- it has **two** parts, physical and mental
- you need to explain how one activity can achieve both of these.

Students have struggled with this topic in recent exams – **be prepared!**   ResultsPlus

Now try this

target B

In a PE theory lesson, Miss Smith explained the reasons for taking part in physical activity.

Complete the table below by identifying one social, one mental and one physical benefit of exercise, for a school student and for someone at work.

Give a different example for each person.   **(6 marks)**

Ensure you read the question carefully.

You need to give a different example in each case.

Type of benefit	Benefit for someone at school taking part in physical activity	Benefit for someone at work taking part in physical activity
Social		
Mental		
Physical		

Mental benefits of an active lifestyle

Regular physical activity can provide mental benefits for individuals.

The 'feel good factor'

Doing exercise makes you feel good by increasing SEROTONIN levels.

Serotonin is a chemical found in the body.

Enjoyment and having fun whilst taking part in physical activity are also MENTAL benefits.

Stress relief

Exercise can help with stress relief.

- It helps you relax.
- It takes your mind off other problems as you focus on the activity.

Worked example

target F

Physical activity can improve your mental health by helping you 'feel good'. Which of the following causes this 'feel good factor'?

(1 mark)

☐ A An increase in testosterone

☒ B An increase in serotonin

☐ C An increase in blood pressure

☐ D An increase in narcotic analgesics

Stress-related illness

Physical activity can help to relieve stress. This means that if you exercise regularly you can reduce the chance of suffering from a STRESS-RELATED ILLNESS, such as depression.

You do not need to remember the names of specific stress-related illnesses.

Increase in self-confidence/self-esteem

Confidence is increased BECAUSE:

- you feel part of something
- you are performing better
- you think you look better

Confidence is increased BY:

becoming a member of a team

practising more

losing weight due to exercise (if previously overweight)

Why and how?

You should always try to match a reason WHY something is achieved with an example of HOW it can be achieved. Always try to match a 'why' with a 'how'.

Now try this

target C

One of the possible benefits of a healthy active lifestyle is an increase in **self-esteem**.

Explain the term self-esteem and provide **one** example of how self-esteem can be increased through physical activity.

(2 marks)

Note that there are two parts to this question. Think about which category of benefit 'self-esteem' is in.

Mental and physical benefits

Some mental benefits occur because taking part in physical activity provides mental stimulation.

Competition

Competition occurs when:

- you try to beat yourself
- you try to beat an opponent.

Examples:

You try to run a certain distance in a faster time than you have before.

You take part in a race to try to beat a rival school team.

Aesthetic appreciation

Aesthetic appreciation is:

- recognising the QUALITY or skill of movement in an activity.

Examples:

You watch a trampolinist perform a routine with perfect body shape.

You watch a rugby player execute a wonderful dodge.

Explaining terms

When asked to explain, don't just repeat the question words. You need to show that you understand their meaning.

Underline key words so that you remember to answer **both** parts of the question. You need to give a specific example of a skilful movement. You could use any physical activity for your answer.

Worked example

target C

Using an example, explain how aesthetic appreciation can be stimulated through physical activity.

(2 marks)

Aesthetic appreciation is recognising the beauty or skill of a movement, for example when playing football you can enjoy seeing a team member demonstrating a high level of skill when they control the ball and kick a perfect volley.

Physical challenge

Physical challenge is something that REALLY PUSHES you OUTSIDE of your comfort zone. This means it challenges you MENTALLY too.

- It might be something you find scary like rock climbing so you are physically AND mentally challenged.
- It might be something so physically demanding, like training for the London Marathon, that you need to be really mentally tough too.

EXAM ALERT!

Physical challenge has both **physical and mental benefits**.

When you see a question on physical challenge, remember:

- it has **two** parts, physical and mental
- you need to explain how one activity can achieve both of these.

Students have struggled with this topic in recent exams – **be prepared!**

ResultsPlus

Now try this

target B

Regular participation in physical activity is considered to be beneficial to the individual.

Explain how participation in physical activity can stimulate **physical challenge**. **(2 marks)**

Good answers include a clear reason as part of an explanation, this could be an example.

3

Fitness benefits of an active lifestyle

The physical benefits of exercise can be about either increasing (physical) fitness or about improving (physical) health. This page focuses on physical fitness benefits.

Physical fitness benefits

Improved physical fitness results from regular exercise and the effects of training.

The fitness benefits are:

- increased strength ⟶ using larger weights with fewer repetitions
- increased muscular endurance ⟶ using the same muscles repeatedly
- increased cardiovascular fitness ⟶ taking part in regular aerobic activity
- increased flexibility ⟶ carrying out mobility exercises and stretching

The fitness benefits are achieved by:

Worked example

target B

Richard is 55 and has just retired from work. He now has more time for physical activity and has chosen to include recreational swimming, cycling and walking as part of his healthy, active lifestyle. Using <u>examples</u>, <u>outline</u> how Richard could gain three different <u>physical</u> benefits through regular participation in these activities.

(3 marks)

Regular participation in these activities is likely to improve his cardiovascular fitness as they are all aerobic activities. He may also improve the muscular endurance in his legs as a result of the cycling and walking. It is also possible his shoulder flexibility could improve as a result of the swimming.

Don't be vague

You might be asked a general question, e.g. Give an example of a physical benefit of taking part in regular exercise.

In this case you could say 'improved fitness for example, increased strength'. Be careful not to be too vague – always say how fitness improves.

- Only give PHYSICAL benefits because that is what the question asks for.
- This response focuses on fitness benefits but could have included physical health benefits as well.
- It is a good idea to give as broad a range of examples as possible with this type of question.

Now try this

target D

Tick the items that are examples of physical fitness benefits of participation in physical activity.

(2 marks)

☐ **A** It makes me feel less tense

☐ **B** It can lead to weight loss if you are overweight

☐ **C** It gives me greater muscle definition

☐ **D** I develop an aesthetic appreciation of my sport

☐ **E** It can improve my confidence

☐ **F** It can increase strength

☐ **G** I enjoy competition

☐ **H** It can improve my physical health

Health benefits of an active lifestyle

Physical health benefits

Improvements in physical health result from regular exercise.

The health benefits include:

- STRONGER bones/REDUCED 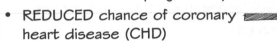 chance of developing osteoporosis
- REDUCED chance of coronary 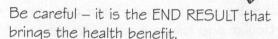 heart disease (CHD)
- REDUCED chance of a stroke ➤
- REDUCED chance of obesity ➤

The improvements are achieved by:

- taking part in weight-bearing activities like running, cycling and walking
- reduced cholesterol / lower blood pressure
- reduced cholesterol / lower blood pressure
- burning excess calories whilst exercising

Be careful – it is the END RESULT that brings the health benefit.

For example, one health benefit from taking regular exercise is a reduced chance of coronary heart disease (CHD). This is as a result of lower cholesterol levels. Note the lower cholesterol level would not be enough on its own.

Weight loss through exercise

The benefits of losing weight can be:

☑ PHYSICAL, e.g. less strain on the heart.

☑ MENTAL, e.g. feeling better about oneself.

Be careful always to explain your answer in the context of being overweight. Losing weight if underweight will damage your health.

Worked example

Complete the table below to explain the long term benefits of regular training. **(3 marks)**

target **B**

Effect	Health benefit
Reduction in resting blood pressure	Reduction in likelihood of suffering from coronary heart disease
Increased bone strength	Reduced chances of suffering from osteoporosis
Weight loss	Only a benefit if previously overweight, less likely to become obese

Make sure that your answers explain the potential benefit to health by naming a specific potential health issue.

Now try this

target **C**

Changes can occur to the body as a result of regular participation in physical activity. One of the benefits of physical activity is that it can improve physical health.

Identify **three** long-term physical health benefits from taking part in physical activity. **(3 marks)**

EXAM ALERT!

Ensure you highlight the key words in the question. Students struggled with identifying three long-term benefits.

This was a real exam question that a lot of students struggled with – **be prepared!**   ResultsPlus

Social benefits of an active lifestyle

It is important to be socially healthy as well as physically and mentally healthy. Someone who is socially healthy can make friends easily and work well with others.

Friendships and social mixing

Joining a club or team is a great way to achieve the social benefits of exercise. These include:

- meeting new people and making new friends
- opportunities to get together with existing friends
- improving cooperation skills
- increased social activities (and therefore will not engage in antisocial behaviour).

Different age groups

Social benefits of an active lifestyle may well vary between different age groups.

For example:

☑ elderly person – getting together with friends as otherwise they may be lonely

☑ child – may see friends at school but needs to develop social skills.

Always be sure to relate your answer to a particular age range if asked to do so.

Worked example

target D

Janice has lost contact with a lot of her friends since leaving school. She has decided to join a local sports club.

Explain how joining a club would help Janice.   **(2 marks)**

If Janice has lost contact with her friends this means she doesn't have any friends to socialise with. By joining a club she has the chance to make new friends.

The question asks you to EXPLAIN.

The first part of the answer identifies Janice's problem based on the scenario in the question.

The second part identifies HOW joining a sports club will help solve the problem.

The importance of cooperating

Cooperation occurs when we work with others and demonstrate teamwork.

Improved cooperation can lead to better understanding of your teammates and better teamwork skills. This may make your team more successful.

Some words are similar, like cooperation, competition and coordination – don't rush!

Always read questions carefully to make sure you are thinking about the right one.

Now try this

target B

Enjoyment is a mental benefit of participation in physical activity.

Explain how the social benefits of participation can lead to increased enjoyment.   **(2 marks)**

Think carefully about the category!

Key influences: people

Many factors impact on being able to sustain involvement in physical activity. The factors are grouped into categories: people, image, culture, resources, health and wellbeing, and socio-economic.

The particular PEOPLE that you must know about are:

- family
- peers
- role models.

There are two important questions about each of these:

WHO is in the category?

HOW do they impact on participation?

Family

Who?

- Parents
- Guardians
- Relations (aunt, uncle, etc.)
- Brothers and sisters

How?

Growing up with family members who take part in physical activities means you are aware of these activities from an early age, e.g. you play tennis because your aunt plays tennis.

Peers

Who?

- Friends
- Classmates
- Other members at your club

How?

Seeing your friends enjoy taking part in activities may make you want to do that activity too.

Role models

Who?

- National and international performers
- Good performers in your school
- People you admire

How?

We all want to be able to perform like someone who is really good. We may start or continue with a sport in order to be like our role model.

Worked example

target **D**

Jennifer is a good all-round sports performer and could represent the school in many different sports but has chosen swimming.

Give **one** way in which her family may influence her choice of sporting activity. **(1 mark)**

If her family are already involved in certain activities she is likely to try those activities as well and therefore continue with them if she is good and enjoys it.

The key point is that when you are younger, if family members play a particular sport, it is likely that you will go with them and also try the sport. They therefore influence the activities you play.

Now try this

target **G**

The performers pictured are related. Player A is David Beckham who plays at elite level, player B is his son Brooklyn who plays for a local club.

Explain **one** likely key influence on Brooklyn's choice of activity. **(2 marks)**

Player A   Player B

7

Key influences: image

Image has an impact on achieving sustained involvement in physical activity. This category includes media and fashion.

Media

The media can have a huge influence on us. We are affected by:

- what we see on tv
- what we read in the newspapers
- what we hear on the radio.

The effect may be positive or negative, depending on the amount of coverage a sport has.

For example:

- there is little coverage of women's sport; therefore fewer girls are influenced by the media to take up sport than boys
- squash is not shown much so people don't think it is worth trying
- football is covered a lot and therefore lots of people see it and want to play.

Fashion

The clothes for some sports are much more fashionable than for others. This can influence which activities we do or don't do.

For example, some people think:

- snowboarding clothes are 'cooler' than skiing clothes
- basketball clothes are more fun than all-white tennis kit.

We are more likely to want to get involved in an activity that has clothing which appeals to us, and that we think makes us look good!

This may be due to how we have been influenced by the media.

Worked example

target C

Image can be a key influence on an individual's choice of whether to participate in physical activity and the activity they choose to participate in.

Give an <u>example</u> of the key influence 'image' and <u>explain</u> why this can influence participation. **(2 marks)**

Fashion is an example. If a sport has really trendy clothes like snowboarding, or a fashionable image, you are more likely to want to be part of that sport rather than a sport that appears boring.

There are two parts to the question; good answers will include an example to support the explanation.

Now try this

target E

The following statements were made by students explaining what influenced them when deciding whether or not to participate in an activity.

Which of the statements below relate to the key influence category 'image'? **(1 mark)**

☐ **A** Whether your friends like the activity

☐ **B** Whether the activity is available to those with disabilities

☐ **C** Whether the local newspaper reports on the activity

☐ **D** Whether you have a long-term illness

Key influences: culture

You need to know about these **four** cultural influences:

1 Age

Your age can influence the activities you do. You often find people of different ages doing different activities.

For example, a 70-year-old man may no longer wish to play rugby due to the nature of the sport but he may still play tennis with his friends.

2 Disability

A person's disability may influence their choice of activity. There are many adapted activities available for people with disabilities, for example wheelchair tennis and wheelchair rugby, and use of sighted guides for visually impaired athletes, but not all activities can be adapted in that way.

3 Gender

Some sports are generally associated with either men or women. For example:

- some men do not want to do dance or play netball as they think of them as female activities
- some women would not play rugby or do boxing as they consider them male activities.

Other influences may be responsible for these thoughts, for example media and fashion in the 'image' category.

4 Race

Some activities are associated more with one race than another. This can be due to:

- influences from the 'people' category, e.g. family or peers influencing whether someone does or does not do an activity
- stereotyping, where people from particular backgrounds are steered towards – or away from – certain activities, e.g. people of African origin being pushed away from swimming and towards long distance running.

Worked example

target **D**

There are <u>cultural</u> key influences that impact on our choice of physical activity.

Which of the following is <u>not</u> an example of a cultural key influence? **(1 mark)**

☐ **A** Age
☐ **B** Disability
☒ **C** Illness
☐ **D** Gender

Try to think of a way of remembering the group of examples in the 'culture' category. For example, C = DRAG (C stands for culture; DRAG is the first letter of each influence in the category).

Now try this

target **B**

Regular participation in physical activity is thought to be beneficial to the individual.

Explain how participation in physical activity can be affected by cultural key influences.

(3 marks)

Key influences: resources

Even if you are good at a sport and enjoy it, without appropriate resources you will not be able to sustain involvement in that activity.

Availability

Is there a suitable club or venue available?

Not all activities are readily available, e.g. windsurfing, mountain biking, hockey. If it's difficult to get to a venue, you will be less likely to participate in that activity.

Even if a club exists there may not be sessions at an appropriate standard, e.g. only beginner sessions, which would be too easy.

Access

Will I be able to get in?

There may be barriers that mean you can't access a venue or activity:

- an AGE requirement to take part
- PHYSICAL barriers, for example no wheelchair ramp or pool hoist
- COST – an expensive activity may mean you have to opt for a cheaper alternative.

Access can overlap with location and socio-economic factors too.

Location

Can I get there?

An activity needs to be available in a place you can get to easily:

- not too far away
- accessible by public transport, so that you don't have to rely on someone to take you.

For example, many more people would ski on a regular basis but there is limited access to mountains or artificial slopes in the UK.

Time

Is the time right for me? And do I have enough time?

- The time of the session needs to be suitable for you, e.g. when you have no other commitments.
- You need to have enough time available, e.g. some activities like golf can take several hours to play.

Worked example

 Target **D**

Some people, for example the tennis player in the image, continue to participate in sport as they get older.

Identify **one** factor that can influence people in sustaining their involvement in physical activity. **(1 mark)**

Resources

Now try this

 target **G**

There are many key influences that impact on our choice of physical activity.

Which category of key influences do the following belong to: access, availability, and time? **(1 mark)**

☐ **A** Socio-economic
☐ **B** Cultural
☐ **C** Resources
☐ **D** Health and wellbeing

If you are not sure, think through the main categories of key influence and you should be able to work out which one these are in.

EXAM ALERT!

About one in four of students selected the wrong category of key influence. Make sure you are one of the students getting this question right by learning the categories of key influences and their examples.

This was a real exam question that a lot of students struggled with – **be prepared!** Results**Plus**

Key influences: health and wellbeing and socio-economic

The ability to sustain involvement in physical activity is dependent on health and affordability.

Health and wellbeing

Someone in good health (physical, mental and social) may be well-motivated to take part in an activity.

Sometimes even a short illness like a cold can prevent us from doing things.

Long-term illnesses and health problems can make continuing any form of physical activity really difficult.

Socio-economic factors

These are the COST and the perceived STATUS of an activity.

- Some activities are relatively inexpensive and are accessible to many people.
- High cost of clothing, memberships and equipment can make it difficult to take part.
- Perceived status – some people may want to take part because they think the activity has a particular status, e.g. golf.

Golden rules

For questions about key influences:

1 Learn the categories of key influence – try to make up a phrase using the initial letters of each category to help remind you of their names.

2 Learn EXAMPLES of each of the categories.

3 Make sure you can explain HOW examples of the category influence participation.

Worked example

Mike is a good all-round sports performer. He plays rugby for the school first team and belongs to a dry-slope ski club, which he attends regularly.

Identify **two** different key influences, other than people or image that could impact on Mike's involvement in sport. **(2 marks)**

Socio-economic and health and wellbeing.

Always make sure you can justify your answer. If you can, you have probably made a good choice.

Try to get into the habit of using the scenario to help you in your choice. For example, skiing is a relatively expensive activity so socio-economic is a good choice. Resources would also have been a good choice as only a limited number of artificial ski slopes are available.

Now try this

Jennifer is a good all-round sports performer and could represent the school in many different sports but has chosen tennis.

Explain how her family's socio-economic status may influence her choice of sporting activity.

(2 marks)

Roles and required qualities

The most obvious role in physical activity is probably that of performer, but many other roles are available. These roles provide additional opportunities for people to become or remain involved in physical activity.

Changing roles

Moving from one role to another can keep people involved in physical activity when they stop playing.

Possible reasons for changing roles include:

- no longer able to play due to an injury
- tried it but didn't like it
- tried it and not good enough to compete but still want to be involved.

Different roles need different qualities.

Leadership (e.g. coach, manager)

Qualities	Explanation
Good organisational skills	To run teams and arrange fixtures / plan sessions
Good communication skills	So people understand exactly what they need to do
Good knowledge of the activity	To plan training sessions appropriate to the activity

Officiating (e.g. referee / umpire)

Qualities	Explanation
Good fitness	To keep up with play
Good communication skills	So people understand decisions
Good levels of confidence	So people are less likely to argue
Good knowledge of the activity	To make the correct decisions

Performer

Qualities	Explanation
Good fitness	To meet the demands of the activity
Good ability	To perform well
Good motivation	To persevere and work hard even if losing

Volunteering (e.g. first aider, club secretary)

A number of roles are filled by people who are volunteers, giving up their time without being paid.

Without volunteers, many clubs would not exist and many sporting events would not happen.

What qualities and why

Always try to say WHY a quality is needed. For example, to say a necessary quality for leadership was 'good leadership' would be too vague, but saying good organisation skills with an explanation as in the tables above would be good.

Now try this

target B

There are a range of roles available in physical activity.

Explain how the range of roles provides opportunities to become, or remain, involved in physical activity.   **(3 marks)**

Note the words 'range', 'become' and 'remain' when answering. Make sure you cover all these points.

Sports participation pyramid 1

The sports participation pyramid is about the numbers of people participating in sport in the UK. You need to be able to explain the pyramid with regard to the foundation, participation, performance and elite stages.

Sports participation pyramid

- The numbers of people participating in sport in the UK are shown by the four stages of the pyramid.

- It gets smaller towards the top – as the level of performance increases, the number of people participating decreases.

- You need to be able to identify each stage from a description or be able to describe each stage.

The four stages of the pyramid

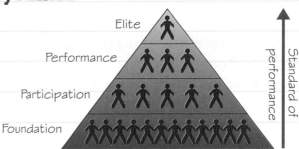

Elite
Performance
Participation
Foundation

Standard of performance

Foundation stage

This is:

- the introductory stage
- at the bottom of the pyramid
- the level that contains the most people
- the level where people start or try an activity, where they only have basic skills
- the level that includes the compulsory sport you do at school.

Participation stage

- You progress to the participation stage when you CHOOSE to continue with sport (when it is non-compulsory), e.g. playing in an after-school club.

- Fewer people are at the participation stage than at the foundation stage.

- Sport is at a slightly higher level of skill than at the foundation stage, but is not as competitive as at the performance stage.

Worked example

target D

As part of an activities week at <u>school</u> Richard <u>tried</u> ice hockey. At which stage would Richard be placed in the sports participation pyramid?

(1 mark)

Foundation level

Use the scenario to work out the answer.

The statement says he TRIED ice hockey, therefore he is being introduced to the activity rather than being someone who plays regularly.

EXAM ALERT!

Many students failed to name a stage. As the question asks for the name of the stage, even correct descriptions cannot be the correct answer.

This was a real exam question that a lot of students struggled with – **be prepared!**

ResultsPlus

Now try this

target D

The image represents the sports participation pyramid, but the names of the stages have been removed and have been replaced by numbers.

Give the correct name for the following stages

(a) Stage 3 **(1 mark)**

(b) Stage 4 **(1 mark)**

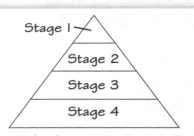

Stage 1
Stage 2
Stage 3
Stage 4

Sports participation pyramid 2

Performance stage

A player at this stage is really good at their sport. Fewer people continue to this stage. It is:

- non-compulsory
- competitive
- where people play in leagues (though not at top levels)
- where skill is improved by coaching and playing in competitions.

Elite stage

The elite (also known as EXCELLENCE) stage of the pyramid is made up of the relatively few performers, who are at national and international levels. Fewer people make it to this stage as it requires a huge amount of skill and determination.

Note that initiatives and agencies (see pages 15 and 16) are all interested in getting more people to progress up the pyramid to reach these higher levels.

Make up a phrase that will help you remember the stages in order, for example:

Feel Positive about Physical Education!

FOUNDATION PARTICIPATION PERFORMANCE ELITE

Getting the terminology right

You must get the term for each stage right, AND get them in the correct order.

There are two letter 'P's, so remember – you have to participate before you can perform.

The pyramid may also be referred to as a triangle.

The stages may also be referred to as levels.

Worked example

target E

Sketch the sports participation pyramid and identify the elite stage.

(2 marks)

Elite

Don't worry if a question asks you to sketch, you don't have to be an artist. Just keep your answer as neat and clear as possible.

This question is worth two marks.

- The top section of the triangle has been identified as the elite stage.
- The triangle has been divided into 4 sections horizontally.

Now try this

target C

Outline why the elite stage of the sports participation pyramid has the smallest number of participants.

(2 marks)

Initiatives and their common purposes

A number of initiatives are set up to encourage people to take part in physical activity and so have a healthier lifestyle.

In order to put these initiatives into practice, specific organisations exist – sometimes called agencies (see next page).

Most of these agencies have similar aims – remember these common aims for your exam:

- increased participation in sport
- retaining people in sport
- creating opportunities for talented performers.

Agencies often target priority groups – these are groups where participation numbers are low, for example the over 50s.

Aim: increase participation

All agencies want to get more people involved in sport and physical activity.

Why?

For the benefits from taking part e.g. increased HEALTH (physical, social and mental) and FITNESS.

Leading to:

- a healthier nation, which is better for everyone – individuals and employers
- more entertainment from better performers.

Aim: retain people

Having started people participating in physical activity the aim is to keep them involved.

Why?

People who remain involved will:

- maintain or improve their fitness and health
- may take on other roles (see page 12)
- are more likely to succeed.

How?

- An effective network of clubs.
- A route to progress with good facilities.
- The opportunity for competition.

Aim: create opportunities

Why?

- For talented performers to achieve success.

How?

- Progression needs to be possible from the foundation to elite stages of the sport participation pyramid.
- Agencies will be involved in supporting this progression, by providing:
  - better facilities
  - better coaching
  - better education.

Worked example

Explain why agencies often target priority groups.   (3 marks)

A common purpose for agencies is to increase participation in sport. Different groups have been identified where participation is generally low, for example the over 50s. By targeting and putting on activities that this group will be interested in they are more likely to get involved and therefore participation rates will increase.

Now try this

Describe a common purpose of initiatives, other than increased participation, developed for getting more people involved in physical activity.   (3 marks)

Note that the question asks you to DESCRIBE, so you will need to do more than just name the purpose.

Agencies

You need to be able to identify agencies involved in providing opportunities for becoming or remaining involved in physical activities. Three agencies are outlined below. Think about how the information about each agency links to one or more of the common purposes from page 15.

Sport England

Working to:

- create a community sport system.

By:

- investing National Lottery Funding
- working with UK Sport (which is responsible for elite success and the Youth Sport Trust)
- delivering a mass participation sporting legacy from the 2012 Olympic and Paralympic Games (Places People Play).

Youth Sport Trust

Working to:

- create a PE and sport system that engages all young people.

By:

- working with schools and National Governing Bodies of Sport to establish new clubs on school sites
- creating the next generation of volunteers as coaches, officials and team managers
- supporting sports colleges.

National Governing Bodies (NGBs)

Working to:

- increase the numbers and skill level of those participating in their sport.

By:

- increasing the quality and quantity of coaches, volunteers and officials
- organising more competitions (at all levels)
- assisting with facility developments.

Most sports have their own NGB, e.g. The Football Association (FA) and Badminton England.

Common aims

All these agencies meet the common aims of:

- increasing and sustaining participation in grassroots sport (the bottom of the sports participation pyramid)
- creating opportunities for people to excel.

Agencies often change due to government directives. Provided you know these three you should be well-prepared for your exam.

Worked example

Identify **three** agencies involved in the provision of opportunities for becoming, or remaining, involved in physical activity.   **(3 marks)**

Sport England
Youth Sport Trust
National Governing Bodies

These are the three agencies you need to know. If the question asked for an example then it would be a good idea to be able to give an example of an initiative that each of these agencies is involved with.

Now try this

Explain the common purposes of initiatives developed by agencies such as Sport England in relation to the provision of physical activities.   **(3 marks)**

The question asks for common purposes, so make sure you give more than one purpose.

Health, fitness and exercise

HEALTH, FITNESS and EXERCISE – you need to know the differences between the terms and the relationship between them.

Definitions

- Questions on health, exercise and fitness often ask you to DEFINE one of the words.
- When asked to define, you need to repeat the exact definition given by Edexcel.
- If the question doesn't ask you to define but to EXPLAIN, you can explain the word in your own words OR use the given definition.

Health

Definition to learn:

'A state of complete mental, physical and social wellbeing and not merely the absence of disease and infirmity.'

You must remember to include all three aspects of health. If one part is missing you are not completely healthy.

Fitness

Definition to learn:

'The ability to meet the demands of the environment.'

In other words you need to be fit enough to do what you need for your everyday life. This is different for everyone – some people only need to be fit enough to work at a desk, others need to be fit enough to complete a manual job.

Exercise

Definition to learn:

'A form of physical activity done to maintain or improve health and / or physical fitness, it is not competitive sport.'

In other words, exercise is something physical that you do in order to keep or improve the other two aspects of a healthy lifestyle – health and fitness.

Worked example

 target C

In order to be a good performer Jared has to be fit. Define the term fitness. **(1 mark)**

Fitness is the ability to meet the demands of the environment.

The question asks you to define, so it is best to give the exact wording given in the glossary of the specification. That way there is no doubt as to whether your answer is correct.

EXAM ALERT!

Only one student in three got this question right. When a question requires a definition, it is best to give the definition that is in the specification glossary to get the mark.

This was a real exam question that a lot of students struggled with – **be prepared!** Results**Plus**

Now try this

 target D

Which of the following statements gives the best definition of health? **(1 mark)**

- ☐ **A** The ability to meet the demands of the environment
- ☐ **B** A state of mental well-being and not merely the absence of disease and infirmity
- ☐ **C** The absence of disease
- ☐ **D** A state of complete mental, physical and social well-being and not merely the absence of disease and infirmity

All options are real definitions related to your course. Make sure you select the option that offers the most accurate and most complete definition.

Health, fitness and exercise and a balanced healthy lifestyle

HEALTH, FITNESS and EXERCISE – you need to be able to relate these terms to a balanced healthy lifestyle and performance in physical activity.

Watch out for the word BALANCED – it often comes up in GCSE PE.

It's about not having too much or too little of one thing, so one of the key factors on the right should never outweigh the others.

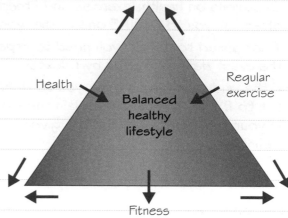

Health → Balanced healthy lifestyle ← Regular exercise

Fitness

Factors working together 😊

To achieve a balanced healthy lifestyle, all three factors need to work together.

For example:

If you take part in regular exercise you can:

- increase your fitness (e.g. muscular endurance and so increase performance too)
- achieve increased health benefits (e.g. reduced chance of CHD).

Regular exercise → Increased fitness → Health benefits →

Factors not working together ☹

If the three factors are not working together, you will not achieve a balanced healthy lifestyle.

For example:

If you are not healthy enough to take part in regular exercise:

- fitness could deteriorate (and so performance will not improve)
- health benefits will not increase.

Note the exercise must be REGULAR to be effective, not just now and again!

Worked example

target B

Which of the following is a true statement about the relationship between exercise, health and fitness and a balanced healthy lifestyle? **(1 mark)**

☐ A You need to be healthy in order to be fit

☐ B If you exercise regularly you can guarantee that you will improve health as well as fitness

☒ C It is possible to be fit but not healthy

☐ D Whatever the intensity, exercise will improve health

First, discount the obvious.

D starts with 'whatever the intensity', which isn't true as it is possible to over-train and cause health issues.

B is false – it makes it more likely, but doesn't guarantee it.

That leaves A or C. Option C is correct – you could be fit but have a temporary illness like a cold, and therefore not be healthy.

Now try this

target A

Explain the relationship between health and exercise.   **(3 marks)**

Cardiovascular fitness and muscular endurance

Cardiovascular fitness and muscular endurance are components of HEALTH-RELATED FITNESS.

Cardiovascular fitness

Cardiovascular fitness is defined as:

'The ability to exercise the entire body for long periods of time without tiring'

> You need both parts – long period of time and without tiring.
>
> Always write cardiovascular rather than the abbreviation CV, to show that you really do know the words.

The cardiovascular system

The cardiovascular system is made up of the heart, blood vessels and blood.

'cardio' = to do with the heart

'vascular' = to do with the blood vessels and the blood they carry.

Together, they supply the body with oxygen to produce energy for exercise.

The better your cardiovascular fitness, the better your oxygen supply will be.

Muscular endurance

Muscular endurance is defined as:

'The ability to use voluntary muscles many times without getting tired.'

Definitions

If you use a definition, make sure it is enough to answer the question. If you are asked to apply or give an example, the definition on its own will not be enough.

Avoiding confusion

Muscular endurance is:

☑ different from cardiovascular fitness – make sure you mention muscles!

☑ different from muscular strength, which is to do with force. 'Endurance' means it has to last a long time without tiring.

Worked example

target **C**

Define the term muscular endurance. **(1 mark)**

The ability to use voluntary muscles many times without getting tired.

EXAM ALERT!

It is important to learn all key definitions. Every year students get definitions wrong because they don't understand the meaning of words.

This was a real exam question that a lot of students struggled with – **be prepared!**

ResultsPlus

Key words to include in your answer: muscles, many times, without tiring.

Now try this

target **D**

As a result of adopting an active lifestyle, an individual may improve aspects of health-related exercise. Which of the following gives the best explanation of cardiovascular fitness? **(1 mark)**

☐ **A** The ability to exercise the muscles of the body for long periods of time without tiring

☐ **B** The ability to exercise the heart and lungs in the body for long periods

☐ **C** The ability to exercise the entire body for long periods of time without tiring

☐ **D** The ability to exercise the entire body for long periods of time

Muscular strength, flexibility and body composition

These are three further aspects of HEALTH-RELATED EXERCISE.

Muscular strength

Muscular strength is defined as:

The amount of force a muscle can exert against a resistance.

It is clearly different from muscular endurance – the emphasis is on exerting as great a force as possible, so by definition it could not be done many times.

Flexibility

Flexibility is defined as:

The range of movement possible at a joint.

Body composition

Body composition is defined as:

The percentage of body weight which is fat, muscle and bone.

You should be able to define or identify a component from its description and to know whether a component is part of health-related exercise or skill-related fitness.

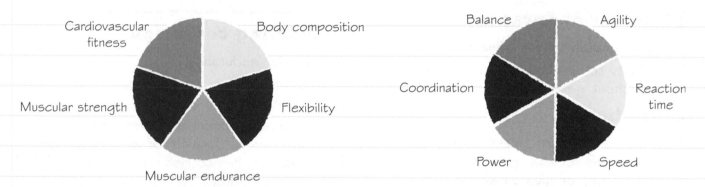

Components of health-related exercise: Cardiovascular fitness, Body composition, Flexibility, Muscular endurance, Muscular strength

Components of skill-related fitness: Balance, Agility, Reaction time, Speed, Power, Coordination

Worked example

target **D**

As a result of regular training it is possible to improve muscular strength. Which of the following is a correct statement about muscular strength? **(1 mark)**

☐ A   The ability to exercise the muscles of the body for long periods of time without tiring

☒ B   The amount of force a muscle can exert against a resistance

☐ C   The amount of force a muscle can repeatedly exert against a resistance without tiring

☐ D   The ability to exercise the muscles of the body for long periods of time

Points A and D both mention long periods of time, so this must relate to muscular endurance. Point C uses the word 'repeatedly' so B must be the correct answer.

Now try this

target **E**

There are five components of health-related exercise. Four of these are listed below.

• Cardiovascular fitness   • Muscular endurance   • Flexibility   • Body composition

Identify the missing component of health-related exercise. **(1 mark)**

Agility, balance and coordination

Agility, balance and coordination are three components of SKILL-RELATED FITNESS. You need to know the effects they will have on your ability to carry out different physical activities.

Agility

Agility is defined as:

The ability to change the position of the body quickly and to control the movement of the whole body.

Examples:

- Players in a rugby team need agility to dodge tackles from the opposition.
- Squash and badminton players should be very agile to quickly change direction, depending on where the ball or shuttle has been played.

Describing agility

The best way to DESCRIBE agility is: To change direction quickly.

It is needed in activities where you are going in one direction and then very quickly change to a different direction, perhaps to avoid an opponent.

You need to include both 'change direction' AND 'quickly' to describe agility accurately.

Balance

Balance is defined as:

The ability to retain the body's centre of mass (gravity) above the base of support with reference to static (stationary), or dynamic (changing), conditions of movement, shape and orientation.

Balance is all about keeping steady to get the best result in performance. There are two types of balance:

Coordination

Coordination is defined as:

The ability to use two or more body parts together.

For example, the body parts that are coordinating could be eyes and hand, as shown here by the tennis player. Good coordination will enable successful contact to be made with the ball.

Dynamic balance (when moving)

Static balance (when stationary)

Coordination of eyes and hand

Worked example

target C

Describe **two** named components of skill-related fitness. **(4 marks)**

Agility and coordination are two components of skill-related fitness. Agility is the ability to change the direction of the body quickly and coordination is the ability to move two or more body parts together.

You are asked to DESCRIBE these components, so a word for word definition is not required as long as you include the key parts: change, direction, quickly, two, and together.

Now try this

target D

Agility is the ability to change the position of the body quickly and to control the movement of the whole body. Explain how balance can aid agility.

(2 marks)

Power, reaction time and speed 1

Power, reaction time and speed are three further aspects of SKILL-RELATED FITNESS. You need to know the effects they will have on your ability to carry out different physical activities.

Power

Power is the ability to do strength performances quickly. So in order to have power, you must have STRENGTH and SPEED.

Most physical activities require a degree of power but here are two examples where power is particularly important.

- A tennis player will need power to serve a ball at 100 mph.
- A high jumper needs power for an explosive lift from the floor to clear the bar.

Reaction time

This is the time it takes to react to a given stimulus. It is particularly important in an event where there is a definite start to a race.

- A Formula 1 driver or a 100-metre sprinter must move immediately when they see or hear the starting lights or gun.

It is important in racket sports and team games.

- A tennis player needs to react very quickly to the shot played by their opponent.
- A football or hockey player needs to decide quickly how to respond to the passes made by team members.

Speed

Speed relates to the amount of time it takes to perform a particular action or cover a particular distance.

- Speed is vital in any race – a runner, cyclist or skater would all depend on speed.
- Speed can be vital for other movements too – a javelin thrower needs to be able to bring their arm through very fast to get the maximum distance with the javelin.

For any aspect of SKILL-RELATED FITNESS, remember to say WHO uses it, HOW they use it and WHY.

Worked example

target C

One component of skill-related fitness is the product of an aspect of health-related exercise and another aspect of skill-related fitness.
Name this component of skill-related fitness.

(1 mark)

Power

Try to work through your answer. You know the answer must be a component of skill-related fitness, so start by making a list of these. Next, decide which one is achieved by combining two other components. You know that power = strength × speed, so power is the correct answer.

Now try this

target D

Define the term 'power' and give an example of its use in a named sport other than weight lifting. **(3 marks)**

You need to write the definitions, state a sport and give an example from that sport.

Effects of cardiovascular fitness and muscular endurance

Cardiovascular fitness and muscular endurance are components of HEALTH-RELATED-EXERCISE. You need to know the effects they will have on your ability to carry out different physical activities.

What, who and how?

When you are thinking about the components of health-related exercise you should ask yourself three questions:

✓ What is it?

✓ Who needs it?

✓ How do they use it?

Cordiovascular fitness

Cardiovascular fitness is required when activities:

- are mainly aerobic
- last a long time
- involve prolonged additional oxygen delivery.

It is used by performers who need to:

- maintain quality of performance over a long time
- work the body for a long period of time WITHOUT TIRING.

Muscular endurance

Muscular endurance is required when activities:

- are mainly aerobic
- last a long time
- require repeated use of the same muscles.

It is used by performers who need:

- prolonged additional oxygen delivery to working muscles
- to repeat muscle contractions over a long period of time WITHOUT TIRING.

Mentioning muscles

When applying muscular endurance you MUST mention the word 'muscles' to show you do not mean cardiovascular fitness.

Worked example

target C

Identify an important component of <u>health-related</u> exercise for a <u>marathon runner</u> and state how this component is <u>used</u> by the marathon runner in their <u>event</u>. **(2 marks)**

The marathon runner would need good cardiovascular fitness. This is used to allow the runner to keep running at a good pace without tiring so they can complete the distance quickly.

For this question you need to:

- identify a component of health-related exercise
- explain how it is useful to a marathon runner.

Cardiovascular fitness and **muscular endurance** are **both important** to a marathon runner so you could use **either** to answer this question.

Now try this

target C

As part of his healthy active lifestyle Ashley trains three times a week on the school track, running at least three kilometres every session. He is improving his cardiovascular fitness and muscular endurance.

Explain the terms '**cardiovascular fitness**' and '**muscular endurance**'. Give an example of how Ashley uses each in his training sessions. **(4 marks)**

Make sure you refer to Ashley's training sessions in your answer.

Effects of muscular strength, flexibility and body composition

Muscular strength, flexibility and body composition are three aspects of HEALTH-RELATED EXERCISE. You need to know the effects they have on your ability to carry out different activities.

Muscular strength

Muscular strength is needed for activities which require FORCE. It should not be confused with POWER. It can be used on its own or combined with speed as an aspect of power.

Who needs it?	How do they use it?
Weight lifter	To lift heavy weights
Gymnast	To support own body weight
Games player	To not get pushed off the ball

Flexibility

Flexibility is important in all activities.

Who needs it?	How do they use it?
Gymnast	Performing splits
Distance runner	For increase in stride length
Hurdler	To achieve hurdling position

Body composition

Body composition will impact on all performers. For example, a sprinter will need a low ratio of body fat to muscle.

Worked example

target
B

Complete the table below by giving an example of how strength would be used by each performer. **(3 marks)**

Performer	How strength is used in their activity
Sprinter	The sprinter would use strength to apply a greater force against the ground or starting block to decrease the time taken to run the race.
Rugby player	A rugby player would use strength to stop himself being barged off the ball, this would allow him to maintain possession.
Weight lifter	A weight lifter would use strength to support a heavy weight above his head at the end of the lift for a short period of time.

Use the phrase 'short period of time' to show that you are talking about strength and **not** muscular endurance. This is an example of the **impact** of strength on performance.

Now try this

target
B

The images below show two performers. Read the statements below and decide which is true.
(1 mark)

Runner　　**Squash player**

☐ **A** Both performers use strength in their performance

☐ **B** Flexibility is not important to the runner

☐ **C** Body composition is not relevant to the squash player

☐ **D** Strength is more important than flexibility to the runner

Effects of agility, balance and coordination

Agility, balance and coordination are three components of SKILL-RELATED FITNESS. You need to know the effects they will have on your ability to carry out different physical activities.

Agility

Agility has two components:

1. The ability to CHANGE DIRECTION.
2. The ability to do so QUICKLY.

It is used by performers that need to dodge to avoid others, for example netball players, basketball players and rugby players.

> Describe agility as the ability to change DIRECTION quickly, not POSITION.

Balance

Balance is used in all activities. But there are some where balance is especially important, e.g.:

- a gymnast uses balance during a handstand to hold his position still
- a discus thrower uses balance as she releases the discus to stay in the throwing circle.

For any aspect of SKILL-RELATED FITNESS, remember to say WHO uses it, HOW they use it, and WHY.

Worked example

Figure 1 shows a woman doing yoga as a form of exercise.

target **D**

Which of the following components of fitness is <u>skill-related</u> and <u>the most</u> important in this yoga pose? **(1 mark)**

☒ **A** Balance
☐ **B** Coordination
☐ **C** Body composition
☐ **D** Strength

All the components are used in this activity, but you need to choose the **most important**.

Coordination

Coordination is important in all activities. Here are three types of coordination.

- HAND-EYE, needed by a tennis player to toss the ball and make contact when serving.
- FOOT-EYE, needed by a football player to watch the ball onto her foot when receiving a pass.
- HAND-HAND, needed by a basketball player to switch hands when dribbling the ball.

You need to make sure it is clear which body parts are working together.

EXAM ALERT!

If an exam question talks about or shows a picture of a specific activity, you will need to apply your answer to this activity. Students often select strength. Remember to select the most important.

This was a real exam question that a lot of students struggled with – **be prepared!**

Now try this

target **C**

Explain the difference between how co-ordination is used by a golfer taking a putt and a swimmer during a 100 m butterfly race. **(4 marks)**

Power, reaction time and speed 2

To show your understanding of skill-related exercise, you need to be able to apply the theory to physical activities. This page is about the application of power, reaction time and speed.

Power

Power is all about using strength at speed, so examples must be of explosive movement.

Who and how?

- Sprinter leaving the starting blocks.
- Gymnast seeking height in a tumbling routine.
- Tennis player serving an ace.
- Basketball player in a jump shot.

Worked example

target **F**

Which of the following components of skill-related fitness would a high jumper require at take off in order to clear the bar?   **(1 mark)**

☐ **A** Agility
☒ **B** Power
☐ **C** Muscular endurance
☐ **D** Reaction time

Reaction time

Fast reactions are useful in events where quick decisions about movements are needed e.g. to get a good start or to adapt quickly to a rapid change in play (normally games situations).

Who and how?

- Rugby player realising the need to change direction due to a deflected ball.
- Badminton player deciding to play a different shot after opponent has 'dummied' their shot.
- Swimmer starting a race as soon as the 'gun' sounds.

Speed

Speed is useful:

- where events are won by the quickest time
- in events where power is needed
- to gain an advantage over opponents e.g. beating them to a loose ball in football.

Who and how?

- 100-metre sprinter – to beat the opponents and get a faster time.
- Marathon runner – in a sprint finish.
- Long jumper in the run up – to jump further.
- Javelin thrower having a fast arm – to increase throwing distance.

Now try this

target **B**

Rank in order the importance of reaction time to performers in the following activities and justify your order.   **(6 marks)**

- Midfielder in a team game
- Gymnast completing a floor routine
- 100-metre sprinter

 6 marks are available here. Place performers in order then justify your choices.

	Order of importance	Justification
1		
2		
3		

Reaction time could be used by any of the performers, so think carefully about which performer needs it the most.

PAR-Q and fitness tests

You need to be able to assess whether you, or someone else, is ready to take part in an exercise programme.

PAR-Q

This is the **Physical Activity Readiness Questionnaire**.

Taking part in physical activity has many health benefits, but for some, taking part might not be appropriate as it could make a current health condition worse.

A PAR-Q is designed to identify any potential health problems that mean physical exercise would not be recommended.

Typical PAR-Q questions

A PAR-Q would include questions about:

- personal physical details (e.g. weight)
- family health history (e.g. any incidence of coronary heart disease)
- known health problems (e.g. high blood pressure)
- lifestyle (e.g. smoking).

Fitness tests

To assess fitness levels in order to develop an appropriate exercise programme, you need to:

- know the fitness requirements for a selection of different activities
- know the tests that measure each of the components of fitness
- be able to interpret the results of the tests
- make recommendations based on the results.

Use of fitness tests

Fitness TESTS should never be part of a training session.

How and why?

Fitness tests are used:

- at the start of an exercise programme
- during a programme to monitor how the training is going
- at the end of the programme to see if it has worked.

Reasons for fitness testing include:

- establishing your current level of fitness
- identifying strengths and weaknesses in fitness
- using this information to plan a relevant training programme
- helping you set SMART targets
- checking for improvements in fitness since the last test.

The student in the picture is completing a questionnaire <u>before</u> undertaking physical activity for the first time at his new club. **(2 marks)**

(a) Name the type of questionnaire the student is most likely to be completing?

PAR-Q

(b) Give an example of a 'typical' question that might be asked on the questionnaire.

Do you smoke? If yes, how many cigarettes do you smoke a day?

There is no need to write 'physical activity readiness questionnaire' in full when answering this type of question.

Explain why family health history is asked for in a PAR-Q. **(2 marks)**

Fitness tests 1

You need to know these **three** fitness tests that measure cardiovascular fitness. This is a component of HEALTH-RELATED EXERCISE.

1 Cooper's 12-minute run test

Test of:

- cardiovascular fitness.

Test used by:

- long-distance runners for endurance activities.

Test protocol:

- Use cones to mark a set distance (e.g. 400 m). Run at a steady pace for 12 minutes.
- Calculate the distance you cover.
- Compare your result to a rating chart.

Group	Excellent	Good	Average	Slow
Boys 13-14	+2700	2400 - 2699	2200 - 2399	2100 - 2199
Girls 13-14	+2000	1900 - 1999	1600 - 1899	1500 - 1599
Boys 15-16	+2800	2500 - 2799	2300 - 2499	2200 - 2299
Girls 15-16	+2100	2000 - 2099	1700 - 1999	1600 - 1699
Boys 17-20	+3000	2700 - 2999	2500 - 2699	2300 - 2499
Girls 17-20	+2300	2100 - 2299	1800 - 2099	1700 - 1799

2 Harvard Step Test

Test of:

- cardiovascular fitness (based on VO_2Max).

Test used by:

- long-distance runners
- for endurance activities.

Test protocol:

- Step up and down on to a specific height box / bench.
- Continue for 5 minutes (1 step every 2 seconds).
- When finished, take your heart rate (HR) immediately – write it down.
- Take your HR again 2 and 3 minutes after completion of the test.
- Compare your result to a rating chart.

3 Treadmill test

(There are several different types of test using a treadmill, e.g. the Bruce Treadmill Test.)

Test of: cardiovascular fitness (based on VO_2Max).

Test used by: Long-distance runners / for endurance activities.

Test protocol:

- Run for as long as you can on a treadmill. Use a standard chart to increase speed and incline by a set amount every three minutes. Record length of time you manage to keep going. Compare your result to a rating chart.

Worked example

target **F**

Which of the following is a test of <u>cardiovascular</u> fitness?   **(1 mark)**

☐ **A** Sergeant Jump test
☐ **B** Sit and reach test
☐ **C** 30-metre sprint test
☒ **D** Harvard Step Test

Reliability

For any test to be reliable it must always be done in exactly the same way and the measurements must be accurate.

Now try this

target **D**

Cooper's 12-minute run test, Harvard Step Test and a treadmill test are all tests of cardiovascular fitness. Name the test which would be most suitable in the following situations.   **(3 marks)**

You may only use each test once.

(a) A large group with access to a school gym who want to test their cardiovascular fitness.

(b) A large group with access to a field, who want to test their cardiovascular fitness.

(c) An individual who wants to test their cardiovascular fitness.

Fitness tests 2

You need to know about these **two** tests which measure different components of HEALTH-RELATED EXERCISE.

① Hand grip test

Test of:

- muscular strength.

Test used by:

- rock climbers.

Validity

Think carefully about WHY you are doing a particular fitness test. This would not be a suitable test to determine the leg strength of a sprinter.

Test protocol:

- Use a grip dynamometer.
- Adjust the grip to fit your hand.
- Keep your arm beside and at a right angle to body.
- Squeeze the handle as hard as you can.
- Compare your result to a rating chart.

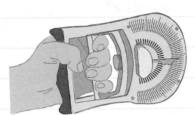

Worked example

target **B**

Discuss the value of the hand grip test for measuring strength relevant to sprinting. **(3 marks)**

The hand grip test is a test of strength so has some relevance, but it is a measure of grip strength not the strength required by sprinters. Therefore it would be better to find a test that related to leg strength for the sprinters.

If a question starts with the word 'Discuss', this normally means that you need to think of good points and bad points relating to the topic and then come to a conclusion at the end. This answer identifies a good point (tests strength), ✓ a bad point (leg strength more relevant to sprinters) ✓ and concludes (look for a test for leg strength) ✓.

---

② Sit and reach test

Test of:

- flexibility (lower back and hamstrings).

Test used by:

- gymnasts
- hurdlers.

Test protocol:

- Use a sit and reach box.
- Sit with legs straight and soles of feet flat against box.
- With palms face down on box top, stretch and reach as far as possible.
- Record distance reached.
- Compare your result to a rating chart.

Now try this

target **C**

The table below shows a rating chart for flexibility scores for the sit and reach test. Explain how this rating chart should be used with a 14-year-old who scored 23 cm in the test. **(3 marks)**

Rating	Age (years)				
	12	13	14	15	16
Good	29	30	33	34	36
Average	26	26	28	30	30
Below average	21	20	23	24	25

Fitness tests 3

You need to know about these **two** tests which measure different component of SKILL-RELATED FITNESS.

1 Illinois Agility Run

Test of:
- agility.

Test used by:
- basketball players
- rugby players.

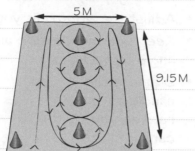

5 M

9.15 M

Test protocol:
- Set up the course as shown in the picture.
- Lie face down on the floor by the first cone.
- On 'GO', run round the course as fast as possible.
- Record the time taken.
- Compare your result to a rating chart.

2 30-metre sprint

Test of:
- speed.

Test used by:
- 100-metre sprinters
- rugby players.

Test protocol:
- Measure and mark out 30 metres in a straight line.
- Place one cone at the start and one at the end.
- On 'GO', run as fast as you can.
- Record the time taken.
- Compare your result to a rating chart.

Worked example

target **G**

Name the fitness test being described below.

Start from a stationary position and when told to 'go', run as fast as possible in a straight line.   **(1 mark)**

30-metre sprint

Most tests will start from a stationary position, so this part of the description doesn't really help. However, the description then says 'run as fast as possible in a straight line'. That implies speed, so it could be the Illinois Agility Run test or the 30-metre sprint. The final part of the description says 'in a straight line' so must be referring to the 30-metre sprint, as the Illinois Agility Run test requires changes in direction.

Now try this

target **C**

Imran plays for the school football team. At the start of the season the team undergoes a series of fitness tests.   **(3 marks)**

In the table below:
- tick the most relevant fitness test for a football player (not goalkeeper)
- explain why this fitness test is relevant to Imran.

Fitness tests	TICK ✓	Explanation: why this fitness test is relevant to Imran
Illinois Agility Run test		
Hand grip test		
Standing stork test		

Fitness tests 4

You need to know about these **two** tests which measure different components of SKILL-RELATED FITNESS.

1 Sargent Jump Test

This is a vertical jump test.

Test of:
- power (legs).

Test used by:
- sprinters
- rugby players.

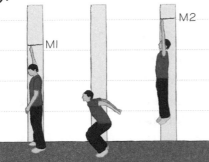

Test protocol:
- Stand side on to a wall, feet flat on the floor.
- Mark the highest point where the tips of your fingers can reach with the arm closest to the wall.
- Holding a piece of chalk in the hand closest to the wall, jump as high as you can (upwards).
- Mark the wall at the top of the jump.
- Measure the difference between the first and second chalk marks.
- Compare your result to a rating chart.

2 Standing broad jump

Test of:
- power (legs).

Test used by:
- sprinters
- rugby players.

Test protocol:
- Stand still, with toes behind a line.
- Jump forwards as far as you can, using a two footed take-off.
- Measure the distance from the start line to the landing point.
- Compare your results to the rating chart.

Worked example

 target **D**

Which of the following is a test of power?

(1 mark)

- ☐ **A** Harvard Step Test
- ☐ **B** Cooper's 12-minute run test
- ☐ **C** 30-metre sprint test
- ☒ **D** Sargent Jump Test

A – test of CV fitness
B – test of CV fitness
C – test of speed
D – power!

With this type of question, go through each option and record next to each what the test measures. This way you know you have selected the correct answer.

Now try this

 target **B**

Describe a test protocol for measuring power in a named test.

(3 marks)

Learn this term!
Students often don't understand the term. It means the procedure for carrying out the test. Highlight or underline the keywords. In this question the key word is 'Describe'.

Fitness tests 5

You need to know about these **three** tests which measure different components of SKILL-RELATED FITNESS.

① Three ball juggle / alternate wall toss test

Test of:

- hand-eye coordination.

Test used by:

- tennis
- netball players.

Test protocol:

- Stand 2 metres away from a wall.
- Throw a tennis ball underarm against the wall.
- Throw with the right hand and catch with the left hand; then alternate hands.
- An assistant counts how many catches you complete in 30 seconds.
- Compare your result to a rating chart.

Although coordination is a very important component of fitness for most activities, there are few tests to measure it. You will need to make your own class rating chart.

② Ruler drop test

Test of:

- reaction time.

Test used by:

- sprinters
- games players.

Test protocol:

- An assistant holds a ruler.
- Stand with your hand open around the ruler at 0 cm.
- The assistant drops the ruler.
- Catch and hold the ruler between thumb and finger, as soon as you can.
- Record how far the ruler dropped (in centimetres).
- Compare your result to a ratings chart.

With sub-maximal tests like this one you should have three attempts and calculate your average. Remember, SUB-MAXIMAL means you are not working flat out, so you do not get exhausted completing these tests.

③ Standing stork test

Test of: balance (static).

Test used by: gymnasts.

Test protocol:

- Place your hands on your hips.
- Place your non-balancing foot against the other knee.
- Raise your heel from the ground so you are balancing on your toes (timing starts when heel lifts).
- Time how long you can hold the balance.
- Compare your results to a rating chart.

Worked example

target **F**

From the list below select the fitness test that would be most appropriate for measuring balance.

- ☐ **A** Harvard Step Test
- ☐ **B** Sargent Jump Test
- ☒ **C** Standing stork test
- ☐ **D** Standing broad jump   **(1 mark)**

If it helps, remember to go through each option and record next to each what the test measures.

Now try this

Name the component of fitness tested by the ruler drop test and describe the procedure for completing it.

(3 marks)

target **C**

Principles of training: progressive overload

You need to be able to describe, explain and apply progressive overload, a principle of training.

Principles of training

No matter how hard you train, the training you do must be appropriate for you to get the maximum benefit from it.

> Here are the key words you will see in examination papers:
>
> Describe – say what it is (could be a definition)
>
> Explain – say how it works
>
> Apply – give examples

> Find a way that works for you to remember the principles. It could be a sentence using the initial letters of each principle. For example:
>
> P=Percy   →   Progressive overload
> S=Skis   Specificity
> I=In   Individual differences / needs
> R=Russia   Rest and recovery
>
> You need to apply all the principles when planning a training programme.

Progressive overload

Progressive overload must show an increase over time and it must be gradual so that no injuries occur.

Description:

Progressive overload means gradually increasing the amount of work in training so that fitness gains occur, but without the potential for injury.

Explanation:

You need to gradually increase intensity in training so that the body continues to increase fitness.

Application:

Week 1 = do 5 sit ups

Week 2 = do 10 sit ups

DON'T confuse the word 'overload' with 'overuse'. You should overload but not overuse, which is forcing yourself beyond your capabilities.

Worked example

target C

Outline the principle of progressive overload, and <u>state</u> how it can improve fitness.   **(2 marks)**

Progressive overload means gradually increasing the work you do. If you increase the work, e.g. you lift heavier weights, you will get stronger, therefore fitter because the body adapts to the new work load.

There needs to be a definition and an example, a link between the principle and why fitness increases. It would not be enough to just say you get stronger.

Now try this

Jamie wanted to improve his cardiovascular fitness by developing a Personal Exercise Programme (PEP) based on continuous training.

Explain how Jamie could use progressive overload to improve his cardiovascular fitness.

   (3 marks)

Principles of training: specificity

You need to be able to describe, explain and apply specificity, a principle of training.

Description:

Specificity means matching training to the particular requirements of an activity.

Explanation:

You must make sure that your training is appropriate for your sport. This is so that you are training the right muscles and body systems, rather than other areas of fitness that will have little impact on your performance.

Application:

For specificity, a rower could plan their training around using a rowing machine.

> Don't get confused with individual needs – specificity is about the requirements of the activity, not the person!

> Using a treadmill instead of a rowing machine may train some of the same things but would not be the best match.

Show your understanding

If you are asked to define or explain specificity, don't just use the word 'specific' in your answer. You need to demonstrate your understanding of the PRINCIPLE of specificity.

Training   Activity

Worked example

 target E

Which of the following statements does <u>not</u> conform to the principle of specificity? **(1 mark)**

☐ **A** A 100 m runner practising their sprint starts

☐ **B** A games player taking part in a fartlek training session

☐ **C** A tennis player practising their first serves

☒ **D** A 50 m freestyle swimmer working on their speed at the track

EXAM ALERT!

Many students failed to gain marks for this type of question because they confused individual differences with specificity. Remember, specificity relates to the needs of the activity.

> Students have struggled with exam questions similar to this – **be prepared!** Results Plus

> The swimmer should be training in the pool rather than on the track.

Now try this

target E

Figure 1 shows three items of fitness training equipment.

Explain which of the items of equipment shown in **Figure 1** is **most** likely to be used by a sprint cyclist. **(3 marks)**

Figure 1

Principles of training: individual differences / rest and recovery

You need to be able to define, describe, explain and apply individual differences and rest and recovery, principles of training.

Individual differences / needs

Description:

This means matching the training to the requirements of the individual person.

> Unlike specificity, individual needs is about the person and not the activity.

Explanation:

It is very important to make sure the training is appropriate for the person, as everyone is different. For example although two people might play the same position in football, if one has higher levels of fitness, they will not benefit from following a fitness programme designed for the less fit player.

Application:

Remmy is 13 and her brother is 16. They both play football. Remmy trains twice a week for 30 minutes, however her brother trains every other day for 60 minutes.

> Note how the training varies because of the differences between the two individuals. The differences in age and sex are likely to mean that Remmy's brother will be physically able to withstand a higher intensity of training, therefore he trains more than his younger sister.

Rest and recovery

Definitions:

REST is the period of time that is allowed for recovery to take place.

RECOVERY is the time required for the repair of damage to the body caused by training or competition.

> If you don't apply this principle, overtraining can occur causing a drop in performance.

Explanation:

Making sure that there is enough time between training sessions so that there is time for adaptations to take place, time for any damage to repair and energy stores to replenish.

Application:

Build a rest day into your training programme. You could also alternate the intensity of the training you do.

Worked example

 target F

Glen is a good gymnast. He is trying to improve by following a training programme based on improving flexibility and speed. Glen's coach has given him a <u>different</u> training programme to the one his friend is following, who is also a gymnast. Why might he do this? **(1 mark)**

Following the principle of individual differences, the coach is making sure the training matches the individual's needs not just the activity.

Now try this

 target A

Describe the training principles of rest and recovery **and** explain why they are important. **(6 marks)**

> If a question is worth six marks, it will require an extended answer. Make sure you highlight key words and plan your answer so that it is balanced and well-written.

35

Principles of training: FITT principle and reversibility

You need to be able to explain the components of the FITT principle: Frequency, Intensity, Time and Type. You also need to be able to explain the term 'reversibility', why it might occur and what its impact on performance might be.

FITT: Frequency

This is about HOW OFTEN you train. It should be gradually increased, for example:

Once a fortnight to start with ➡ Once a week ➡ Twice a week

Training more often can lead to improved performance.

FITT: Intensity

This is about HOW HARD you train. It should be gradually increased for example:

- 1 set of 5 repetitions of a 5 kg weight
- 2 sets of 5 repetitions of a 5 kg weight
- 2 sets of 5 repetitions of a 10 kg weight.

Training harder can lead to improved performance.

FITT: Time

This is about HOW LONG you train. It should be gradually increased, for example:

Session 1 = 20 minutes ➡ Session 2 = 25 minutes ➡ Session 3 = 30 minutes

Training for longer can lead to improved performance.

FITT: Type

This relates to specificity. The closer the match between the type of training and the activity, the better the improvement in performance.

Worked example

target C

As part of her practical exam, Jackie was asked how she applied the FITT principle in her PEP.

Describe how Jackie could apply one of the components of the FITT principle.

(1 mark)

Jackie could increase the frequency of her training. She may have started training once a week and increased it to twice a week in the second week of her PEP.

Overlap with other principles

The FITT components should be taken into account when applying progressive overload, but remember to apply the principle of rest and recovery too!

Reversibility

This means that any improvement or change that takes place as a consequence of training, will be reversed when you stop training.

Just as fitness can be increased through training, the benefits will be lost if training stops due to injury or a holiday.

Now try this

target C

The FITT principle of training is made up of four parts. Which of the following statement covers all four parts? **(1 mark)**

☐ **A** How hard and often you work, making sure you do not do too much, whilst avoiding boredom

☐ **B** How long, hard and often you work, whilst maintaining safety

☐ **C** How hard and often you work, making sure that your training fits the requirements of the activity, and that you do not do too much

☐ **D** How long, hard and often you work, making sure that your training fits the requirements of the activity

Values of goal setting and SMART targets

You need to be able to explain the VALUES of goal setting and describe, explain and apply the principles of setting SMART targets.

Values of goal setting

Examples of the values of setting goals are:

Increased:

- motivation and feel-good factor
- focus
- standard.

Improved:

- monitoring of progress
- planning of training sessions (due to focus).

All these values can lead to improved performance.

SMART targets

In order for the goals you set to be successful, you need to use SMART targets. You need to apply all of them.

SMART stands for:

S = SPECIFIC

M = MEASURABLE

A = ACHIEVABLE

R = REALISTIC

T = TIME BOUND

Specific ⓈMART

Description:

Your goal must be clear (specific).

Explanation:

A vague idea (e.g. 'I must get better') is NOT specific or clear enough to provide the focus you need to bring about improved performance.

Application:

A specific and therefore clear target is:

To reduce the percentage of unforced errors in my passing from the centre third in netball.

Just saying 'to improve in netball' is too vague.

Measurable SⓂART

Description:

In order to know if your goal has been met successfully, it must be something that can be measured.

Explanation:

The best way to measure something is to have units of measurement, for example time, distances, numbers. Then you can measure if the target has been achieved.

Application:

When giving examples of a measurable target make sure it has a number in it, for example:

To run 10 k __3 seconds__ faster than my previous best.

Just saying 'to run a 10 k race faster' is too vague.

Worked example

target D

Target setting should apply the principle SMART. What does the letter __S__ represent in the acronym SMART **and** why is it important when setting targets? **(1 mark)**

The letter S stands for Specific – it is important to make sure that your target is clear so you know what you are aiming for.

Now try this

target G

Teachers use the SMART principle to help you set effective targets.

Why do targets need to be measurable? **(1 mark)**

SMART targets

SMART targets must also be Achievable, Realistic and Time-bound.

Achievable   S M (A) R T

Description:

An achievable target means it is something that it is possible for you to do.

Explanation:

You need to avoid setting targets which would be too difficult for someone to complete. This would be demotivating, therefore it is important that a performer has the ability, with training, to reach the targets set.

Application:

I currently run 100 m in 14.30 seconds. My goal is to run 100 m in 14.20 seconds.

Realistic   S M A (R) T

Description:

A realistic goal is one that is possible, given all the factors involved.

Explanation:

Your goal might be achievable but are the other factors in place that make it realistic? For example, do you have access to training facilities, and do you have the time required?

Application:

I currently throw the javelin 30 m, I am going to start an additional training session each week and my goal is to throw 35 m by the end of this season.

Time-bound   S M A R (T)

Description:

Goals must be assigned a time frame for completion.

Explanation:

You need to have a cut-off point by which you should have achieved your goal, so that you can see if your training is having the effect you want.

Application:

My goal is to run 200 m in 45 seconds by the 4th July this year.

Goals can be given a broad time line, which may be:

- short term
- medium term
- long term.

You may have several short-term goals which are leading towards a long-term goal.

For example:

My SMART goal is: I currently average a goal a match in hockey. With additional practice I aim to average 2 goals per match by 30th December.

Worked example

target C

Targets for sports performers should be achievable and time-bound. Complete the table below by describing:

- one consequence of setting unachievable goals. **(1 mark)**
- one advantage of setting goals that are time-bound. **(1 mark)**

Consequence of setting unachievable goals	Performer would get demotivated and therefore stop training causing a drop in performance rather than an increase
Advantage of setting goals that are time-bound	Performer has a clear date to have achieved goal by so maintains motivation to complete it and beat the deadline

Now try this

target F

Teachers will set targets with you to help you improve in all aspects of physical education. They will use the SMART principle to help you set effective targets.

The S of SMART stands for Specific, the M stands for Measurable and the T stands for Time-bound.

What does the letter R of SMART stand for? **(1 mark)**

Interval training

You need to be able to describe the methods of training and explain how they can improve health and fitness. You should also be able to select the most appropriate method for the requirements of a range of specific activities.

Characteristics

This type of training has periods of intense activity, with breaks within the session to allow recovery.

A typical session is usually made up of:

- sets of high intensity work (e.g. sprint)
- followed by rest or low intensity work (active rest)
- followed by high intensity work (e.g. sprint)
- followed by rest or low intensity work (active rest).

Aerobic and anaerobic

Aerobic – 'with oxygen' (low intensity, longer duration activities)

Anaerobic – 'without oxygen' (short lived, explosive activities)

Benefits

- Aerobic interval training will have the health benefits associated with this type of activity, e.g. weight loss (if overweight) due to burning calories.
- It is a very flexible training method that can be used to improve health and fitness in a range of ways.
- Although normally associated with powerful and explosive activities, it can be adapted to work on cardiovascular fitness by altering the lengths of the rest periods.

If you are asked to name a method of training to improve cardiovascular fitness, only use interval training if you can CLEARLY justify your answer by explaining how it can be adapted.

Forms of interval training

These include:

- training on a track
- circuit training
- weight training.

Although interval training can be designed for both aerobic and anaerobic activity, it is usually associated with shorter anaerobic events like sprinting and is a major form of training for swimmers.

Interval training methods can be designed so that most components of fitness can be improved through an interval training programme. Strength could be improved if breaks are programmed in to a weight training session, for example:

- 10 reps arms, rest arms
- 10 reps legs, rest legs
- 10 reps arms, rest arms.

Worked example

Explain how you could tell by looking at a performer's <u>interval training</u> session plan if they were an endurance or power athlete. **(2 marks)**

Fewer rest intervals for an endurance athlete than for a power athlete and less intense workload during period of work for an endurance athlete compared to a power athlete.

Make sure you make it clear which type of performer you are talking about.

Now try this

Interval training is a method of training that can be used by a variety of performers.

Describe three characteristics of interval training. **(3 marks)**

'Characteristics' means things that are specific to that method of training.

Continuous training

Training can be interval or continuous. This page looks at continuous training.

Characteristics

In continuous training, each training session must:

- be (preferably) for 20 minutes or longer
- not involve any breaks during the session.

For example:

Run at a steady pace around a 400-metre track for 30 minutes (without stopping).

Benefits

Components of health-related exercise that would improve with continuous training:

- cardiovascular fitness
- muscular endurance.

Regular continuous training can reduce the chance of coronary heart disease.

ALL methods of training if done on a regular basis over a period of time will bring about fitness adaptations, for example:

- lower resting heart rate
- decreased recovery time.

Aerobic or anaerobic

You need to know which methods of training should be used to develop fitness for aerobic activities, and which for anaerobic activities.

- Interval training is used more for anaerobic activities.
- Continuous training is aerobic and is therefore used more for aerobic endurance-based activities.

Aerobic activities are SUB-MAXIMAL. This means you do not work flat out and so can continue to work for long periods of time.

Activities associated with continuous training

- ☑ Long-distance running
- ☑ Long-distance cycling
- ☑ Long-distance swimming

Worked example

target G

What type of activity would an athlete probably be involved in, if they only used <u>continuous training</u> to improve their fitness? **(1 mark)**

They are likely to be involved in an endurance event, for example marathon running.

Remember that 'athlete' is a term that can be used to mean any sports performer, not just those participating in 'athletics'.

Now try this

target C

Why would a long-distance runner use continuous training as their main training method? **(2 marks)**

Fartlek training

Fartlek training is a form of CONTINUOUS TRAINING. Its key CHARACTERISTICS are variations in pace and terrain covered.

Key benefits

 Jogging (aerobic)

 Sprinting (anaerobic)

Changes of pace allow for recovery so performer can work maximally.

Fartlek training improves cardiovascular fitness and muscular endurance and reduces the chance of coronary heart disease.

Fartlek training is continuous, but the changes in pace within the sessions mean that performers work both aerobically (jogging) and anaerobically (sprinting, running uphill) within the exercise session.

Activities associated with fartlek training

(Netball)　(Hockey)　(Rugby)　(Basketball)

This is due to the similarity between the training method and the game situation where there is sprinting and recovery, e.g. making a fast break in hockey and then jogging back into position.

Worked example

 target B

Some training activities can be **adapted** to suit different performance activities. How might a <u>cross-country runner</u> and a <u>footballer</u> <u>adapt</u> fartlek training to suit their own activity? **(2 marks)**

A cross-country runner would focus on changing terrains, e.g. up and down hills.

A footballer would focus on variation in pace to match game requirements.

EXAM ALERT!

Many students found this question difficult because they didn't read the question carefully. Instead of saying how the training session was adapted, they just explained the training method.
Make sure you read all questions carefully.

This was a real exam question that a lot of students struggled with – **be prepared!** ResultsPlus

Now try this

 target E

Why should you involve jogging and sprinting in a fartlek session, if you are a games player?　**(2 marks)**

Think about what a games player does during the game.

Circuit training

Circuit training involves a chain of different activities that can be selected to suit individual or activity requirements.

Can be used to develop all of the components of fitness depending on the nature of the stations included, e.g.
- sit ups for muscular endurance
- shuttle runs for speed
- dodging through cones for agility
- balancing ball for balance.

There are a number of stations (usually between 6 and 12).

The stations are organised in a circuit, so that you can progress from one station to the next.

The stations can be fitness or skill based.

Can be organised so that it is continuous, usually done with 30–60 second breaks while leaving one station and getting in position at the next – INTERVAL TRAINING.

Characteristics and benefits of circuit training

The variety of stations allows recovery of muscle groups (so anaerobic work is possible).

Aerobic circuit training will have the health benefits associated with this type of activity, e.g. weight loss if overweight through burning additional calories.

The intensity can be measured by:
- the TIME at each station
- the NUMBER OF REPETITIONS at each station
- the NUMBER OF CIRCUITS completed.

Depending on the intensity of the activity, circuit training can be aerobic (low intensity) or anaerobic (high intensity).

Worked example

target F

George is 15 years old. He has designed a circuit to help improve his performance in basketball and badminton.

Four of the circuit stations are listed below:

(2 marks)

   Station 1 – running in and out of cones

   Station 2 – lay-up shots using a basketball and basketball ring

   Station 3 – bowling at a target

   Station 4 – badminton serves.

Explain why one of these <u>stations</u> is not appropriate for George's circuit.

Station 3, bowling at a target, does not relate to either of his sports.

Now try this

target D

Outline **three** characteristics of circuit training.

(3 marks)

Weight training

Characteristics of weight training

The key characteristics are:

- a form of INTERVAL TRAINING using weights
- involves 'reps and sets'. The weights are lifted a number of times (reps), followed by a break before starting another set
- weight provides a resistance or load for the muscles to work against.

Using weight training

Weight training can be completed by using machines or free weights.

The muscles you wish to train can be targeted by doing specific exercises, for example, biceps curls work on the biceps!

Benefits

Weight training can be used to develop fitness for many activities, the most obvious being those requiring POWER and STRENGTH.

For example:

- weight lifting
- rugby
- shot putt.

It can also be used for activities requiring MUSCULAR ENDURANCE, for example tennis.

The components of fitness developed due to weight training depend on the design of your training session.

For example:

- to develop POWER and STRENGTH use high weight × low number of reps
- to develop MUSCULAR ENDURANCE use low weight × high number of reps.

Worked example

target D

Ria has taken up <u>discus</u> and wants to know what training method to use to help improve her performance. Explain which <u>training method</u> she should use. **(2 marks)**

Weight training – as this will help her increase her strength so she can throw the discus further.

Make sure you answer **both** parts of the question. If you can justify your choice, you know you must have made a good decision.

Now try this

target B

Endurance and power athletes will often use weight training as part of their training programme.

Describe how weight training can be used to develop muscular strength or muscular endurance.

(2 marks)

Cross training

Cross training is a method of training that uses a combination of other types of training.

Characteristics of cross training

Cross training uses more than one type of training.

For example

- fartlek training on Tuesdays
- circuit training on Thursdays
- weight training on Saturdays.

Its characteristics therefore depend on the types of training being used.

Benefits

Cross training is useful if you take part in:

- more than one activity
- an activity that is made up of different types of events.

It can be used to:

- improve all round fitness.
- add variety to training and therefore keep you motivated to continue.

Performers who benefit from cross training

- Triathletes
- Pentathletes
- Heptathletes

The heptathlon is made up of seven events:

- 100-metre hurdles, 200-metre, 800-metre
- shot putt, javelin
- long jump, high jump.

The fitness demands of high jump are very different from those of shot or the 800 m, so a combination of training methods is needed to collectively meet the demands of the sport.

The fitness benefits gained depend on which types of training you are using.

For example, a combination of weight training and interval training could be used to increase:

- muscular strength
- speed
- power.

Rest

Appropriate rest still needs to be built into a cross training programme. It is not enough just to change method of training, as there will not be time for muscle repair or training adaptations.

Worked example

Give **two** advantages of cross training.   **(2 marks)**

Gives variety to training by using a combination of training methods so the performer doesn't get bored. It also provides an opportunity to train for a range of activities, for example, for a heptathlete who has to train for seven different events.

Two advantages are given and an example is used to support the answer.

Now try this

target D

Which of the following methods of training would be most suitable for a triathlete?   **(1 mark)**

☐ A   Weight training
☐ B   Cross training
☐ C   Continuous training
☐ D   Interval training

Think about what a triathlete needs to do in their event.

Exercise session: warm-up

Any exercise session should be broken up into three separate phases: a WARM-UP, the MAIN EXERCISE SESSION and a COOL-DOWN. The main exercise session and cool-down are dealt with on page 46.

Structure of a warm-up

The warm-up itself also has three stages:

1. a pulse raiser
2. stretching
3. drills specific to your activity.

You must know about all three stages and the order in which they occur.

Examples of activities at each stage are:

1. Pulse raiser, e.g. jogging, this speeds up oxygen delivery to the working muscles.
2. Stretching – stretching the muscles you are about to use to help prevent injury.
3. Drills – more intense practices relating to the main session, for example, dribbling a basketball if you are about to play basketball.

A good warm up can take a minimum of 10 minutes, and probably much longer.

Reasons for the warm-up

The benefits of a good warm-up are extensive.

• It physically and mentally prepares you for exercise.
• It increases oxygen delivery to the working muscles.
• It increases the temperature of muscles, tendons and ligaments reducing the chance of injury.
• It increases flexibility, which will aid performance.

The drills you do should mimic those you are about to use in the main session, in order to:
☑ help prepare muscles
☑ focus your mind
☑ rehearse the skills you are about to use.

Worked example

target **F**

State three phases of a warm-up.

(3 marks)

1. Pulse raise
2. Stretching
3. More intense exercise / drill related to the main session

Make sure you state the phases in the correct order.

EXAM ALERT!

Students sometimes get confused by the term 'phases'. Make sure you give the three different phases, rather than examples of them.

This was a real exam question that a lot of students struggled with – **be prepared!**

Now try this

target **D**

Three of the following statements relate to warm-ups and their purpose. Which statement does not?

(1 mark)

☐　**A**　The pulse raiser section of the warm-up increases the amount of oxygen transported around the body

☐　**B**　The warm-up decreases the amount of lactic acid present and therefore reduces the likelihood of muscle soreness after the activity has finished

☐　**C**　The warm-up gets the performer mentally ready for the activity, as well as physically ready

☐　**D**　The warm-up increases the temperature of the body, resulting in it being better prepared for activity

Exercise session: main session and cool-down

The MAIN SESSION and the COOL-DOWN are the second and third phases of an exercise session.

The purpose of the main session

- If the main session is a match or an event, then the purpose will be to put your training and targets in to practice.

- If the main session is part of your training programme, then the purpose will be to work on the areas of skill or fitness you have planned.

Structure of a cool-down

There are two stages of a cool-down:

1. Light exercise, e.g. slow jogging, at a much lower intensity than you have just been working.

2. Stretching – stretch the muscles you have used in the main activity.

A cool-down is NOT designed to prevent injury – you should not get injured at this stage as you have finished the main session and will be reducing the intensity of the work.

Reasons for the cool-down

There are many benefits from a cool-down:

- aids the removal of lactic acid, which can build up in the muscles making them feel stiff and sore

- aids the removal of carbon dioxide and other waste products

- helps bring the heart rate and breathing rate SLOWLY back down to their resting rates

- helps avoid dizziness due to blood pooling in the lower limbs which can happen if you suddenly stop exercising

- improves flexibility.

Worked example

target G

Which of the following statements is a benefit of a cool-down? **(1 mark)**

- ☐ **A** It increases lactic acid production.
- ☒ **B** It reduces the risk of muscle stiffness after exercise.
- ☐ **C** It <u>further</u> increases blood flow to the muscles after exercise.
- ☐ **D** It reduces the chance of injury <u>during</u> the activity.

Option A isn't a benefit and is clearly incorrect, however C and D could be thought correct if you only read the question quickly. Be careful to read all the words in each statement – the words underlined in C and D should show you these are incorrect answers.

EXAM ALERT!

Remember, you can cross through incorrect answers on the question paper as you work through the multiple-choice questions.

This was a real exam question that a lot of students struggled with – **be prepared!**   Results Plus

Now try this

target E

Choose words from the box below to complete the following statements about the cool-down phase of an exercise session. **(6 marks)**

This takes place .... exercise. It is made up of .... phases. To begin with, the performer might carry out some light .... followed by .... Effective cool-downs can reduce muscle .... and increase muscle ....

> tension, after, strength, two, sprinting, during, four, skills, stretching, jogging, soreness, flexibility

Exercise session: endurance

You need to be able to plan and present examples from typical training sessions, that will match the fitness needs of particular individuals or activities.

The warm-up and cool-down have not been included on this plan, just the main session, but you need to include full details when designing your sessions.

SPECIFICITY:
The performer is a games player who wants to improve their endurance, they apply the principle of specificity by using fartlek training where the change of pace matches the requirement of their sport.

REST AND RECOVERY:
Training is not on consecutive days and therefore allows for rest and recovery to take place.

Session plan to improve ENDURANCE

Aim: To work towards my target of being able to run continuously for the whole of my football match (90 minutes) without losing quality of performance.

Target end date February 28th.

Week 1	M	20 minutes fartlek running (0 hills)
	T	Rest
	W	Rest
	T	25 minutes on treadmill (0 incline)
	F	Rest
	S	Rest
	S	Rest

Week 2	M	25 minutes fartlek running (2 hills)
	T	Rest
	W	Rest
	T	35 minutes on treadmill (1 incline)
	F	Rest
	S	Rest
	S	30 minutes fartlek (2 hills)

Week 3	M	30 minutes fartlek running (3 hills)
	T	Rest
	W	40 minutes on treadmill (1 incline)
	T	Rest
	F	35 minutes fartlek running (3 hills)
	S	Rest
	S	40 minutes on treadmill (1.5 incline)

PROGRESSIVE OVERLOAD:
The intensity of the training session is gradually getting harder but not by too much at a time. For example, in Week 2 the time and the incline on the treadmill show a small increase.

INDIVIDUAL NEEDS:
The training has been designed for the performer's own SMART target.

FITT:
F – The number of sessions each week is increasing.

I – The sessions are getting harder.

T – The sessions are getting longer.

T – Fartlek sessions match the activity.

(FITT = Frequency, Intensity, Time and Type)

Now try this

target D

Look at the extract from a training log below and decide whether the performer is training to improve their endurance or power. Explain the reasons for your answer.   **(3 marks)**

Remember the best answers include justification.

Task	Length of time on each task
Warm-up by light jog at 40% maximum pace	5 minutes
Jog at 50% maximum pace	4 minutes
Jog at 60% maximum pace	8 minutes
Jog at 50% maximum pace	4 minutes
Cool-down	5 minutes
Total training time	26 minutes

Exercise session: power

You need to be able to plan and present examples from typical training sessions, that will match the fitness needs of particular individuals or activities.

The warm-up and cool-down have not been included on this plan but you need to include full details when designing your sessions.

SPECIFICITY:
The performer is a sprinter who wants to improve their speed. They apply the principle of specificity by using training that works on the main muscles used in sprinting. They also do short sprints, which matches the requirement of their sport.

REST AND RECOVERY:
Training is not on consecutive days and therefore allows for rest and recovery to take place.

Session plan to improve POWER

Aim: To sprint 100 m in 15 seconds by 31st August. My current PB is 15.60 secs.

Main session

Week 1

Mon 30 mins	3 sets x 5 squat jumps
	3 x 5 push-ups with claps
	3 x 20 m sprint
Tue and Wed Rest	
Thur 30 mins	4 sets x 5 squat jumps
	4 x 5 push-ups with claps
	3 x 20 m sprint
Fri, Sat and Sun – Rest	

Week 2

Mon 40 mins	5 sets x 5 squat jumps
	5 x 5 push-ups with claps
	5 x 20 m sprint
	3 x 5 sets 1 leg calf raises (l then r)
Tue and Wed Rest	
Thur 40 mins	4 sets x 5 squat jumps
	4 x 5 push-ups with claps
	3 x 20 m sprint
Fri, Sat and Sun – Rest	
Sun 45 mins	5 sets x 5 squat jumps
	5 x 5 push-ups with claps
	4 x 20 m sprint
	4 x 5 sets 1 leg calf raises (l then r)
	3 x hopping ladder drill

Week 3 = repeat week 2

PROGRESSIVE OVERLOAD:
The intensity of the training session is gradually getting harder but not by too much at a time. For example, although there is an increase from Week 1 to Week 2, in Week 3 they repeat Week 2 sessions (Week 4 would show further increases).

INDIVIDUAL NEEDS:
The training has been designed for the performers own SMART target.

FITT:

F – Number of sessions each week is increasing.

I – The sessions are getting harder.

T – The sessions are getting longer.

T – Sessions match activity.

(FITT = Frequency, Intensity, Time and Type)

Now try this

Look at the extract from a training log below and decide whether the performer is training to improve their endurance or their power. Explain the reasons for your answer. **(3 marks)**

Task	Time / Number of repetitions
Warm up by light jog at 40% maximum pace	5 minutes
Run 30 m at 85% maximum speed then walk to recover	10 repetitions
Run 80 m at 85% maximum speed then walk to recover	4 repetitions

Heart rates and graphs

You need to know the terms associated with heart rate and exercise and you need to be able to plot heart rates on a graph and evaluate the results.

Explanation of terms

You need to understand the following terms in relation to exercise.

RESTING HEART RATE

This is your heart rate when at rest.

WORKING HEART RATE

This is your heart rate during exercise.

RECOVERY RATE

This is the time it takes for your heart rate to return to your resting heart rate after exercise. The fitter you are, the quicker this happens.

Drawing graphs

- Always use a pencil to plot a graph.
- Don't use a ruler for a line graph as the line should be flowing from one point to the next rather than stopping.
- Make sure you choose the correct type of graph. A graph to show heart rates at several points during the same session would be shown using a line graph not a bar chart as they connect to each other rather than standing alone.

Worked example

target D

The heart rate monitors in the image below show three different heart rate values.

(a) Re-order these values and plot a graph to show the performer's resting, working and recovery heart rate. **(2 marks)**

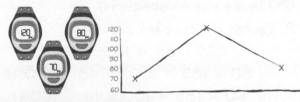

EXAM ALERT!

Many students struggled to explain recovery rate and did not use a line graph. If you are asked to draw a graph of a heart rate make sure you choose the right one.

This was a real exam question that a lot of students struggled with – **be prepared!**   Results Plus

(b) Explain why you have plotted the heart rate values in this order. **(2 marks)**

Watch 1 shows the highest value so this must be when the performer is working – this is their working heart rate.

Watch 2 shows the lowest value so this must be when the performer is resting – this is their resting heart rate.

Watch 3 has a value just higher than the resting heart rate watch. It can't be resting as it is higher than resting, but it is not high enough to be working. Therefore this must be the recovery heart rate.

You are required to explain, so clear information is needed.
Note how the line does not go below the values.

Now try this

target C

Heart rate values for three students at rest, during and after exercise

(a) Which student had the lowest resting heart rate? **(1 mark)**

(b) Whose pulse rate increased the most during exercise? **(1 mark)**

(c) Which student recovered from exercise the quickest? **(1 mark)**

Use the information in the graph to guide you.

Setting training target zones

You need to use graphs to demonstrate and explain target zones and training thresholds.

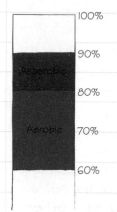

Training within your target zone

- To maximise the chance of fitness adaptations taking place, you should train within your target zone.

The area of the target zone you aim to work within depends upon the intensity of your activity or the aim of your training programme.

If your activity has lots of high intensity work, you should aim to work nearer the upper threshold of your target zone.

Your anaerobic training zone is:

- 80 to 90% of your max heart rate (MHR).

If your activity is mainly low intensity or you wish to use fat as an energy source, you should aim to work nearer the lower threshold of your target zone.

Your aerobic training zone is:

- 60 to 80% of your (MHR).

To estimate your target zones

Your starting number is always 220.

220 minus your age (or any age you are given) this gives you a MHR.

Then calculate 80% and 60% of your MHR.

You will have two HR figures: 80% is the upper threshold of your aerobic training and 60% is the lower threshold of your aerobic training zone.

Examples:

1. Bobbie is 16 years old

     220 − 16 = 204   (MHR)

   80 × 204 ÷ 100 = 163   (80%)

   60 × 204 ÷ 100 = 122   (60%)

You can round figures up and down, so Bobbie's training zone is between 160 and 120 beats per minute (bpm).

2. Lauren is 35 years old

     220 − 35 = 185   (MHR)

   80 × 185 ÷ 100 = 148   (80%)

   60 × 185 ÷ 100 = 111   (60%)

Her training zone is between 150 and 110 bpm.

Worked example

target B

If the correct target zone for an endurance athlete is 120–160 bpm, how old is the athlete?

(1 mark)

☐ **A** 15   ☒ **B** 20   ☐ **C** 25   ☐ **D** 40

You would need to use the target heart rate calculation to answer this question. 220 − age = maximum HR.

220 − 20 = 200

60% of 200 is 120 bpm

80% of 200 is 160 bpm

Now try this

target B

State which of the lines on the graph in Figure 1 (A, B, C or D) would indicate that Sulliman (aged 16) was working within his target zone whilst training? **(1 mark)**

Use the information in the graph to guide you, and remember that there should be an upper and a lower limit to a target zone.

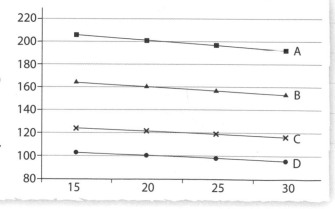

Requirements of a balanced diet

You need to understand the link between exercise, diet, work and rest, and to be able to explain what makes a balanced diet.

Explaining a balanced diet

- A balanced diet means eating the right foods, in the right amounts. This will enable us to work and exercise properly.

- If we don't eat a variety of foods in the correct proportions, we will not get all of the macronutrients and micronutrients we need to make up a balanced diet.

Diet is what you eat on a day-to-day basis and should not be confused with 'being on a diet'.

See pages 52 and 53 for an explanation of macronutrients and micronutrients.

The 'eat well' plate shows how we need to make up our diet from different types of food to get the correct balance.

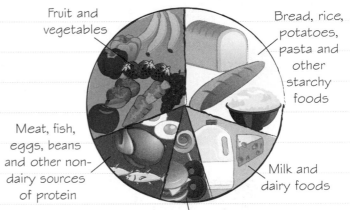

Fruit and vegetables

Bread, rice, potatoes, pasta and other starchy foods

Meat, fish, eggs, beans and other non-dairy sources of protein

Milk and dairy foods

Food and drinks high in fat and / or sugar

Variety as well as balance

You need a balance of food from the different groups and a variety from within each group.

For example, the 'eat well' plate shows we should have a high proportion of fruit and vegetables. The recommendation is that we eat '5 a day', but variety within the group is still important to make sure we get the necessary range of nutrients. This is why eating 5 apples will only count as ONE of your '5 a day'.

Input vs output

Although we need a balanced diet the QUANTITY we need (the input) relates to how much exercise we do (the output).

Health problems can occur:

- if we eat too much in relation to the amount of activity we do (can become overweight).

Or:

- if we eat too little in relation to the amount of activity we do (can become underweight).

Worked example

target C

Jenny was trying to improve her diet, to make it more <u>balanced</u>.

(a) Describe the term '**balanced diet**'.
(2 marks)

A balanced diet means eating a variety of foods from all the different groups of food in the correct proportions.

(b) Give **one** reason why it is important to have a balanced diet. (1 mark)

Without a balanced diet we will not get all the nutrients we need so we may become ill or lack the energy we need for work and exercise.

Now try this

target B

Diet is an important factor to consider when planning for a healthy, active lifestyle.

State **one** possible consequence of a poor diet. (1 mark)

Note that this question is about health, not fitness.

Macronutrients

A nutrient is something that gives nourishment to the body. 'Macro' is the opposite of 'micro' and means things on a large scale. Macronutrients are the nutrients that we need to have in our diet in large quantities. We need them for ENERGY, GROWTH and REPAIR. Everyone needs them, but those involved in physical activity will need more of them. There are three main types of macronutrients.

Carbohydrates

- Contained in bread, pasta, potatoes, rice.
- Should be eaten in greater quantities than the other macronutrients.
- Provide us with energy for use in aerobic and anaerobic activity.

Fats

- Contained in butter, oil, fatty meats and fried food.
- Should form the smallest percentage of macronutrients in diet.
- Provide us with energy but should be eaten in moderation.
- Easily stored in the body and can lead to weight gain.

Proteins
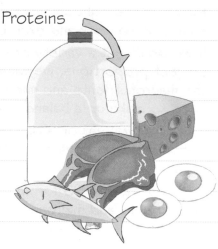

- Contained in cheese, milk, eggs, lean meat, fish.
- Used for growth and repair of the muscles.
- Can produce energy but this is not their main function.
- May be used by performers such as sprinters, to aid muscle growth (hypertrophy).

Worked example

target G

Fats and carbohydrates provide performers with energy.

(a) Which macronutrient should you eat a <u>larger amount</u> of, fat or carbohydrate? **(1 mark)**

Carbohydrate

(b) Why is this food type a <u>better source</u> of energy for you? **(1 mark)**

It can be used in either aerobic or anaerobic activity.

EXAM ALERT!

Macronutrients and micronutrients are easily confused – learn these terms.

Exam questions similar to this have proved especially tricky in the past – **be prepared!**

Now try this

target D

1 Give **one** reason why you need to consider what you eat if you exercise regularly. **(1 mark)**

target C

2 Explain the use of macronutrients in maintaining a healthy, active lifestyle. **(4 marks)**

 Think about what your body needs when you exercise.

Micronutrients

You need to explain the importance, and use, of micronutrients.

Micronutrients are the nutrients that we need to have in our diet in small quantities.

- Minerals and vitamins are micronutrients.
- We need them to maintain good health. Everyone needs them but those involved in physical activity will need more of them.
- Minerals and vitamins are found in the food we eat but some foods have more than others.
- Our body can store some for future use but some cannot be stored and so we need to eat a fresh supply every day.

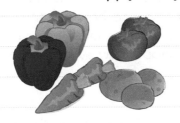

Minerals and vitamins

- There are many different vitamins and minerals.
- Each vitamin or mineral is good for different things. For example, you will often hear people talking about Vitamin C helping to keep you healthy and free from colds.
- Vitamins and minerals can help with your immune system, as well as with general health and growth.
- Vitamins are found in fresh fruit and vegetables.
- Minerals are found in lots of different foods, including meat and vegetables.

Specific micronutrients to note

VITAMIN D

Vitamin D is found in dairy foods, such as milk, cheese and eggs and helps the body absorb the mineral calcium.

CALCIUM

Calcium is a mineral found in foods such as milk and other dairy products. One of its functions is to help keep our bones strong.

Water and fibre

Water and fibre are not nutrients, but they are still essential components of a balanced diet.

WATER

Water prevents dehydration and is in most liquids and many foods.

FIBRE

Fibre aids the digestive system and is found in foods such as cereals, vegetables and nuts.

Worked example

target **E**

The following should all be present in a balanced diet. Which of them aids bone development?   **(1 mark)**

☐ **A** Fibre   ☐ **C** Carbohydrates

☒ **B** Minerals   ☐ **D** Proteins

A specific mineral is not given, but it is the mineral calcium that aids bone development.

Now try this

target **D**

The lists below give different combinations of important nutritional requirements of a balanced diet. Which of them does NOT include a micronutrient?   **(1 mark)**

☐ **A** Fibre, Water, Vitamin A, Carbohydrates   ☐ **B** Water, Fibre, Carbohydrates, Fats

☐ **C** Carbohydrates, Calcium, Protein, Fibre   ☐ **D** Protein, Fats, Vitamin A, Vitamin C

Had a look ☐   Nearly there ☐   Nailed it! ☐

Timing of dietary intake

You need to eat to provide energy for exercise. However, WHEN YOU EAT in relation to WHEN YOU EXERCISE is very important. Dieticians work with top athletes to help them calculate what to eat and when to eat it, so that they get optimal energy levels for performance.

How long to eat before exercising

For an average-sized meal you should leave at least 2 hours before exercising

It can take up to 4 hours to fully digest a large meal – the bigger the meal, the longer it will take to digest

Increased blood supply

There may be a problem about blood supply if you eat too close to exercising.

- When you eat, you need an increased blood flow to the digestive system to aid the process of digestion.
- When you exercise, you need an increased blood flow to the working muscles to provide additional oxygen and nutrients.

A conflict occurs if you eat just before exercising because both areas (digestive system and working muscles) cannot have an increased blood flow at the same time.

Why the timing is important

- Undigested food that remains in the stomach during exercise can cause discomfort and even lead to you feeling nauseous.
- The digestive system breaks down the food we eat into smaller components. We can then use these smaller components for providing energy.
- If digestion is not complete, we might not have the required amount of energy we need.

Worked example

target D

Planning what and when you eat is an important part of leading a healthy, active lifestyle. Which of the following would be the most appropriate amount of time to leave <u>before</u> exercising, after a <u>large meal</u>? **(1 mark)**

☐ A No need to wait as food will provide essential energy

☐ B Five minutes

☐ C Half an hour

☒ D Over an hour

Note the reference in the question to a large meal. It would take the body at least two hours to digest a large meal, so D is the only possible answer.

EXAM ALERT!

Look for answers which are obviously wrong in multiple choice questions first, and cross them through. Once you have reduced it to two options, go for the more obvious, considering the key words (here, 'a large meal').

This was a real exam question that a lot of students struggled with – **be prepared!** ResultsPlus

Now try this

target B

During exercise, blood flow to parts of the body changes. Explain why a performer should consider the timing of dietary intake because of changes to blood flow.

(4 marks)

Redistribution of blood flow

You need to be able to explain the redistribution of blood flow (blood shunting) during exercise.

When you exercise your working muscles need more oxygen. Oxygen is attached to the red blood cells in the blood and carried to your active muscles.

Your heart rate and stroke volume increases so more blood is circulating every minute.

Blood is diverted away from inactive areas to the working muscles. This is called BLOOD SHUNTING.

Blood can be shunted away from the stomach. This is why is is important that digestion is complete before exercise begins.

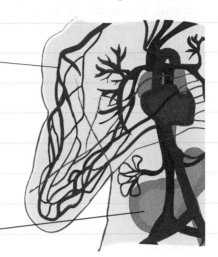

Vasoconstriction

- Vasoconstriction means that the blood vessels are constricted (squeezed) to make them smaller.
- When you start to exercise, chemical changes trigger signals from your nervous system.
- These signals cause the blood vessels that supply the INACTIVE areas (e.g. the digestive system) to CONSTRICT, reducing blood flow to these areas.

Vasodilation

- Vasodilation means that the blood vessels are dilated to make them bigger.
- When you start to exercise, chemical changes trigger signals from your nervous system.
- These signals cause the blood vessels that supply the ACTIVE areas (the working muscles) to DILATE, increasing blood flow to these areas. This means that these muscles receive more oxygen and nutrients.

Worked example

Using the words in the table below, complete the following statements about blood flow whilst at rest and during physical activity.

target **D**

unchanged	equal
lower	greater

Blood flow to the digestive system is __greater__ at rest than when exercising.　**(1 mark)**

Blood flow to the muscular system is __lower__ at rest than when exercising.　**(1 mark)**

Now try this

target **D**

Using the words in the table below, complete the following:　**(2 marks)**

Reduced blood flow to specific areas of the body is achieved through ....

The need for .... to the muscles during exercise means that performers need to consider the timing of their dietary intake so that performance is not negatively affected.

blood shunting	digestion
cardiac output	increased blood flow

Mesomorphs

There are three extreme body types. The classification of different body types is known as somatotyping. You need to be able to describe the different somatotypes and explain the effect each can have on participation and performance.

Somatotypes

- This is the term used for describing different body types or an individual's physical build.
- It is generally thought that having a certain body type makes you more suited to some activities than others.
- There are three extreme body types:
  - mesomorph
  - ectomorph
  - endomorph.

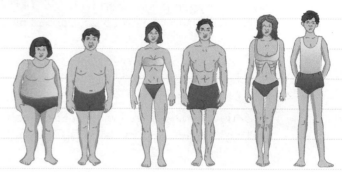

You only need to know these three categories of somatotypes. Most people are actually somewhere in between these extreme body types.

Mesomorph

Key characteristics are:
- low levels of fat
- builds muscle easily
- solid build
- wide shoulders
- narrow hips.

Individuals with an extreme mesomorph body type are suited to activities requiring power, speed or strength, for example:
- sprinting
- weight lifting
- boxing.

Worked example

target **G**

Name the <u>body type</u> of the performer in the image. **(1 mark)**

Mesomorph

This performer needs power to compete their event. For power, you need to be muscular so a mesomorph body type is an advantage in sprinting.

Now try this

target **F**

1 State **one** reason why a mesomorph body type is an advantage in tennis. **(1 mark)**

2 Other than sprinting and playing tennis, identify an activity where having a mesomorph body type would be an advantage. **(1 mark)**

Ectomorphs and endomorphs

Ectomorphs and endomorphs are two of the three extreme body types you need to know about.

Ectomorph

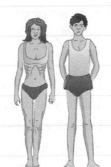

Key characteristics are:

- long, thin frame
- narrow shoulders and hips
- slim build
- generally does not build muscle easily
- generally does not store fat easily.

Individuals with an extreme ectomorph body type are suited to activities where being light is an advantage, as there is not too much weight to carry or lift, for example:

- long distance running
- high jump.

A high jumper will also benefit from being tall.

Endomorph

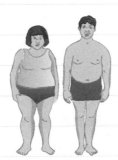

Key characteristics are:

- wide hips
- narrow shoulders
- has a tendency to store fat.

Individuals with an extreme endomorph body type are suited to some activities requiring power or where added weight is an advantage.

They can use their bulk to add momentum to throws, or can overpower or resist opponents, for example:

- shot putt
- sumo wrestling
- some positions in rugby (e.g. props).

Worked example

target **G**

Name the <u>body type</u> of the performer in the image. **(1 mark)**

Ectomorph

Now try this

target **E**

1   Give an example of when an endomorph body type would be an advantage in physical activity.

(1 mark)

target **B**

2   Explain the effect on performance in long distance running of having an endomorph body type. **(3 marks)**

It is an advantage for anyone who needs to lift their own body weight in their event, to be relatively light. The ectomorph body type is therefore well suited to high jumping.

Factors affecting optimum weight

You need to be able to outline why and how, optimum weight varies and to explain how this may affect participation, and performance, in physical activity.

'Optimum weight' means the ideal weight someone should be, based on their:

- height
- sex.

By using these two factors, you can find an estimated ideal range that your weight should be between.

Many ELITE performers would be considered to be over the optimum weight, due to other factors such as:

- bone structure
- muscle girth.

Therefore, these factors also need to be considered when deciding optimum weight.

Height

How tall you are will affect your weight – the taller you are, the more you may weigh.

Height can be an advantage in activities:

- where you need to outreach your opponent, for example basketball
- when the use of longer levers may be beneficial, for example bowling in cricket.

Suggested optimum weight should only be used as a guideline, as it will vary due to height, sex, bone structure and muscle girth.

Sex

Whether you are male or female can make a difference to your weight. Males tend to have more muscle mass and therefore weigh more. This provides men with an advantage in activities requiring strength or power. Males and females compete separately in activities of this sort, for example athletics.

Muscle girth

This is the size of the muscle, its circumference. People with bigger muscles will weigh more. Bigger muscles are generally an advantage in activities requiring speed, power and strength, such as throwing a javelin.

Bone structure

Some people have longer or wider bones than others and will also have greater bone density.

Someone with a larger bone structure will weigh more than someone of the same height with a smaller bone structure. Bone strength is important in many activities, in particular contact sports such as rugby.

✓ These factors may influence the activities we do. It doesn't mean you can't play basketball if you are small, just that someone who is taller may have a natural advantage.

✓ Some activities, like boxing, have specific weight categories.

Worked example

State **three** factors that will affect optimum weight.　　**(3 marks)**

1　The height of the individual: the taller they are the more they will weigh.
2　How much muscle they have: the greater their muscle girth the more they will weigh.
3　The sex of the individual: men tend to weigh more than women.

Now try this

What impact does bone structure have on optimum weight?　　**(1 mark)**

Anorexia and underweight

You need to be able to explain the terms 'anorexic' and 'underweight' and explain how they may impact on achieving sustained involvement in physical activity.

Anorexia nervosa

Anorexia nervosa is a very serious eating disorder. The sufferer refuses to eat due to an obsessive wish to lose weight.

The body will lack all the nutrients supplied by a healthy balanced diet. This can result in:

- fatigue
- fainting / dizziness
- dehydration
- muscular atrophy (reduction in muscle size)
- death.

Be careful when answering questions about the benefits of exercise. DO NOT say that one of the benefits is to lose weight without justifying it clearly by adding 'if overweight'. Losing too much weight is a potentially serious health issue.

Underweight

The term 'underweight' means not weighing as much as expected for your height and sex.

Remember that expected weight ranges are a guide and that there are other factors to be taken into account (see page 58).

It is not healthy to be underweight, just as it is not healthy to be overweight.

Impact on physical activity

- Being anorexic or being very underweight will lead to serious health issues. There will also be an impact on achieving sustained involvement in physical activity.
- If you become too tired or weak to take part in physical activity your fitness and performance levels will clearly deteriorate.

Worked example

target G

Planning what you eat is an important part of leading a healthy, active lifestyle. Which of the following is considered to be the most <u>dangerous to our health</u>? **(1 mark)**

(BEING ANOREXIC)   (BEING OVERWEIGHT)   (BEING OVERFAT)

Being anorexic

Now try this

target C

Give **two** reasons why is it unlikely that an individual who has a healthy lifestyle will become anorexic. **(2 marks)**

Overweight, overfat, obese

These are three terms that you need to know when talking about people who have excess weight. You should use these terms and avoid saying that someone is fat, which is too vague.

Overweight

- The term 'overweight' means that you weigh more than the expected weight for your height and sex.

- You can be overweight while not being overfat.

- Being overweight is not in itself harmful – unless it is accompanied by also being overfat.

Some top performers will be overweight due to other factors, e.g. muscle girth and bone density, but they do not have excess fat.

Overfat

The term 'overfat' means you have more body fat than you should have. If the level of fat in the body is excessive, it can lead to health problems, for example:

- high blood pressure
- high cholesterol levels.

Note that it is possible to be overfat but not actually be overweight.

Obese

'Obese' is a term used to describe people who are very overfat. This is where the body fat has increased to a level that is seriously unhealthy (not just being a few pounds overweight). High levels of excess fat can lead to:

- mobility issues / lack of flexibility
- additional stress on bones and joints
- heart disease
- type 2 diabetes
- depression due to low self-esteem.

The impact on sustained involvement

In addition to the serious health issues of being obese, overfat or very overweight, there will also be an impact on achieving sustained involvement in physical activity.

- ☑ Some of the resulting health problems, e.g. heart disease, will prevent any strenuous physical activity.

- ☑ If you become too tired, immobile, or have difficulty in walking or running, this will affect your ability to take part in physical activity.

Worked example

Explain the difference between being overfat and being overweight. **(3 marks)**

target D

Overfat means having more body fat than you should have, overweight means weighing more than you should. This could be due to being overfat or it could be due to additional muscle mass, therefore being overweight does not necessarily relate to having too much fat but being overfat does.

Now try this

target C

1 Identify **two** physical health risks associated with being obese. **(2 marks)**

2 Explain **one** impact of being overfat on achieving sustained involvement in physical activity. **(3 marks)**

target A

Anabolic steroids

Many types of anabolic steroids have the same chemical structure as the male hormone testosterone. This is produced naturally by the body, but performers increase the amount they have by taking artificially-produced versions of it.

To allow them to train harder for longer, so increasing POWER and STRENGTH

To increase protein synthesis, helping to develop lean muscle mass.

Reasons athletes take anabolic steroids

To speed up recovery time

To increase their chances of winning

Due to pressure from others

Health risk and cheating

There are lots of good reasons NOT to take performance-enhancing drugs. Using performance-enhancing drugs in competition is CHEATING.

There are also significant health risks, including:

- liver damage, CHD
- testicular atrophy, which leads to a decrease in sperm count (infertility)
- skin problems, including acne
- mood swings, including increased aggression
- premature baldness.

Who might use anabolic steroids?

Anabolic steroids could provide an advantage in activities requiring POWER, like sprinting or weight lifting.

Sprinter Ben Johnson was disqualified from the Olympic 100-metre final in 1988 after testing positive for anabolic steroids.

Worked example

Rank these performers in order; so that the one <u>most</u> likely to use <u>anabolic steroids</u> is listed first, the one least likely is listed last. **(1 mark)**

- Tennis player
- Long distance runner
- Sprinter

Sprinter, tennis player, long distance runner

This rank order is based on the relative importance of power and strength to each of the performers. The more important they are, the more 'attractive' taking steroids becomes.

Now try this

Identify **two** possible health risks of taking anabolic steroids. **(2 marks)**

Beta blockers

Beta blockers are drugs that are designed to treat various health issues, particularly those associated with the heart such as high blood pressure. They work by blocking the effects of adrenaline, so helping slow down the heart rate.

They have a calming effect

They reduce the performer's anxiety

Reasons performers might take beta blockers

They reduce muscle tremor or shaking

They allow the performer to remain in control

They increase the chances of winning

Health risks associated with beta blockers

Reported side effects of beta blockers include:

- slowing heart rate (therefore oxygen delivery, therefore drop in performance in endurance events)
- lowering of blood pressure
- sleep disturbance leading to tiredness.

As beta blockers work with chemicals that occur naturally within the body and they are quickly absorbed, it can be hard to detect them when testing for banned drugs.

Who might use beta blockers?

Use of beta blockers could be an advantage in any activity that depends on PRECISION, for example:

- archery
- target shooting
- gymnastics
- diving.

Worked example

target
E

Which of the following is a known effect of <u>beta blockers</u> on health?   **(1 mark)**

☐ **A** Nausea and vomiting
☐ **B** Dehydration
☒ **C** Tiredness
☐ **D** Loss of balance

Now try this

target
E

Some participants take illegal performance enhancing drugs to control their heart rate, despite the obvious health risks.

What effect do beta blockers have on a participant's heart rate?   **(1 mark)**

Diuretics

Diuretics are drugs that increase the rate of urination, so increasing the amount of fluid the body loses. Unlike other performance-enhancing drugs, diuretics are not banned because they directly enhance performance, but because of other potential benefits.

To achieve quick weight loss (due to loss of fluid from the body)

Reasons performers might take diuretics

To mask or hide other performance-enhancing substances the performer may have taken, making them harder to detect

Health risks associated with diuretics

Reported side effects of diuretics include:

- dehydration
- nausea, headaches
- heart / kidney failure.

If you are asked about the side-effects of drugs, don't refer to 'heart problems' or 'kidney problems', as they are too vague.

Who might use diuretics?

Diuretic use could be an advantage in any activity with a weight category or where it is a benefit to be light, for example:

- boxing
- horse racing (jockey).

It could also be useful to any performer trying to mask other performance-enhancing drugs.

Worked example

Give an example of a performer who may take diuretics in order to achieve quick (but temporary) weight loss.

target **G**

(1 mark)

Boxer

Boxers have to be within certain weight categories before they are allowed to compete.

EXAM ALERT!

Do give the obvious answer – make sure you focus on what's being asked and don't overcomplicate your answer.

Exam questions similar to this have proved especially tricky in the past – **be prepared!**

 Results Plus

Now try this

target **G**

Which of these categories of drugs is used to hide the presence of other performance-enhancing drugs? **(1 mark)**

- ☐ **A** Anabolic steroids
- ☐ **B** Stimulants
- ☐ **C** Diuretics
- ☐ **D** Narcotic analgesics

You may be able to answer some multiple choice questions without looking at the options given. If you know the answer to the question without needing to look at the options, this is a good way of checking your answer.

Narcotic analgesics

Narcotic analgesics were designed to relieve pain temporarily. They act on the brain and spinal cord to dampen the effect of painful stimuli, thus masking pain.

They increase the performer's pain threshold

They give a sense of euphoria

Reasons performers might take narcotic analgesics

They mask injuries so the performer can continue to compete

They give a sense of being invincible

Health risks associated with narcotic analgesics

Reported side effects include:

- nausea / sickness
- anxiety / depression
- kidney / liver damage
- addiction
- concentration loss
- further damage to injury (due to masking of pain).

Who might use narcotic analgesics?

Activities where performers might risk using narcotic analgesics include:

- sprinting
- boxing
- football
- swimming.

In fact, ANY performer with an injury who wishes to carry on training and performing could be tempted to take this category of drug.

Worked example

When might a performer be tempted to take narcotic analgesics?   **(1 mark)**

When they have an injury but need to continue to train.

EXAM ALERT!

Always read the question carefully – remember that narcotic analgesics are pain killers.

Exam questions similar to this have proved especially tricky in the past – **be prepared!**

 Results Plus

Now try this

When injured, some performers may be tempted to take drugs to allow them to maintain their training.

What category of drug would a performer take to mask or hide pain?   **(1 mark)**

Make sure you know the reasons why performers are tempted to take performance-enhancing drugs.

Stimulants

Stimulants are a category of drugs that temporarily elevate mood. They increase brain activity, making an individual feel more awake and alert, and as if they have more energy. The taking of stimulants in large enough quantities constitutes the use of performance-enhancing drugs and is therefore banned.

To increase alertness (mental and physical) so the performer is quicker to respond

To increase levels of aggression

Reasons performers might take stimulants

To reduce tiredness

To increase competitiveness

To increase heart rate (and therefore oxygen delivery)

Health risks associated with stimulants

Reported side-effects of stimulants include:

- insomnia
- anxiety
- aggression
- heart rate irregularities.

Facts about stimulants

☑ Stimulants are found in everyday products that contain caffeine, e.g. coffee and many soft drinks. However, you are unlikely to reach banned levels of caffeine simply through drinking these!

☑ Stimulants can be used to treat anything from a cold to ADHD.

☑ Amphetamines are one of the most common stimulants that are used illegally.

Who might use stimulants?

There are two main areas where stimulants might appeal to performers.

1. Where an increase in AGGRESSION would be helpful. It helps to have a certain level of aggression in very physical sports as the performer is more prepared to take the 'physical knocks', for example:
   - rugby
   - boxing
   - ice hockey.

2. Where the performer needs to stay ALERT over a long period of time, for example:
   - long-distance cycling
   - baseball.

Worked example

target **C**

Which of the following is a known effect of stimulants on health? **(1 mark)**

☐ A Nausea and vomiting
☐ B Dehydration
☒ C Irregular and increased heart rate
☐ D Loss of balance

Consider all options and make sure your choice is the best from those available.

Now try this

target **C**

Describe the circumstances that might lead to a performer taking stimulants, even though they are a banned performance-enhancing drug. **(2 marks)**

Peptide hormones

Peptide hormones are found naturally in the human body. They increase muscle growth and increase the red blood cell count.

Examples of peptide hormones are:

- Human Growth Hormone (HGH)
- Erythropoietin (EPO).

 EPO is one occasion where you can write an abbreviation in your exam paper!

Reasons performers might take peptide hormones

| Human Growth Hormone (HGH) – can help increase muscle mass and therefore strength | Erythropoietin (EPO) – can help increase red blood cell production and therefore increase oxygen delivery to working muscles. |

Health risks associated with peptide hormones

Reported side effects of peptide hormones include:

HGH
- arthritis
- heart failure
- abnormal growth in feet and hands
- diabetes

EPO
- increased thickness of the blood
- blood clots / strokes / deep vein thrombosis
- increased risk of heart attack

Who might use peptide hormones?

Activities where performers might risk using peptide hormones include:

HGH

Any activity where an increase in STRENGTH would be helpful, for example:
- sprinting
- weight lifting.

EPO

Any activity where an increase in OXYGEN delivery would be helpful, for example:
- rugby
- distance running
- distance cycling.

Worked example

 target G

In an attempt to improve performance, some participants will resort to taking performance-enhancing drugs. If a performer takes Erythropoietin (EPO), what type of activity are they likely to compete in? **(1 mark)**

An endurance event like long-distance running.

Now try this

target B

How does Erythropoietin (EPO) aid performance in long-distance runners? **(3 marks)**

Recreational drugs

Recreational drugs are those taken for ENJOYMENT rather than to enhance performance. They can be ADDICTIVE and certainly DAMAGE HEALTH. The most commonly used recreational drugs are alcohol and nicotine (cigarettes).

Negative effects on health

ALCOHOL

Heart failure

Increased blood pressure

Increased weight

Liver disease / cancer

NICOTINE

Strokes

Bronchitis

Heart disease / angina

Blood clots

Emphysema

Lung cancer

Negative effects on performance

ALCOHOL

- Leads to slower reaction times.
- Makes the drinker less mobile due to excess weight.
- Causes loss of coordination.
- Causes loss of concentration.

These effects will have a negative impact on performance in ALL activities, whether aerobic or anaerobic.

NICOTINE

- Causes breathlessness.
- Reduces oxygen-carrying capacity.

These effects will have a negative impact on performance in ALL aerobic or endurance-based activities.

Worked example

target **D**

Smoking does not form part of a healthy lifestyle. Identify two of the possible negative effects of smoking on the cardiovascular system. **(2 marks)**

Smoking can lead to heart attack or strokes.

Look out for questions where a specific area of health has been identified, in this case the *cardiovascular* system. Make sure you write about the correct system.

Now try this

target **E**

Identify **two** of the possible negative effects of smoking on the respiratory system. **(2 marks)**

The question asks you to focus on the effects on the *respiratory* system.

Reducing risk through personal readiness

Many physical activities have risks associated with them. You need to be able to identify those risks and know how to reduce them.

General and specific risks

- There are GENERAL RISKS associated with most physical activity. For example, you could sprain an ankle or pull a muscle in most activities.

- There are also ACTIVITY-SPECIFIC RISKS. For example, the risk of being hit with a hockey stick is specific to hockey.

You need to be able to identify and reduce all these risks. To do this do the following:

1. Make a list of all the possible things that could happen in an activity.
2. Decide on a way of reducing each of the risks you have identified.

Example – hockey

Look at these examples of risks associated with playing hockey.

1. Heart attack
2. Shin splints
3. Pulled muscle
4. Fractured shin
5. Broken tooth

Each of these risks can be reduced through PERSONAL READINESS.

Reducing risk through personal readiness

Here is how you would reduce each of these risks:

1. Complete a PAR-Q.
2. Allow recovery time.
3. Warm up.
4. Use the correct clothing.
5. Apply the rules of the game correctly.

Then you need to explain HOW each measure will reduce the risk:

1. To identify any potential health risks and limit participation accordingly.
2. To prevent over-use injury.
3. To prevent injury, e.g. pulled muscle.
4. Wear shin pads to provide padding.
5. Don't lift hockey stick above shoulder so teeth are not hit.

Worked example

target D

Which of the following statements gives the <u>most</u> important reason for wearing the correct clothing when taking part in physical activity?   **(1 mark)**

☐ **A** It gives you the opportunity to look good.

☐ **B** It gives you a psychological advantage over the opposition.

☒ **C** It reduces the chance of injury.

☐ **D** It is in the rules of physical activity.

Always watch for the word 'most'. Other statements may be true but are not the MOST important.

Now try this

target C

Complete the table below by giving examples of how personal readiness can reduce each potential sports injury. Use a different example for each one.   **(2 marks)**

Potential sports injury	Example of risk reduction through personal readiness
Fractured shin	
Soft tissue injury	

Reducing risk through other measures

As well as checking personal readiness for an activity, there are other measures that should be taken to reduce risk.

If you consider the risks associated with rugby, you might identify the following as possible injuries:

1. crush injury
2. dislocated shoulder
3. gash on leg.

Sometimes questions state an activity and ask you to identify the risks – but other times you are asked to choose the activity. If you are, make sure you choose an activity that has obvious risks. For example, it's easier to talk about risks associated with rugby than table tennis.

Here are the OTHER MEASURES you could use to reduce the three risks identified above:

1. Make sure the competition is balanced.
2. Check the equipment.
3. Check the facilities.

Here are examples of HOW each measure could be used to reduce the risk:

1. Avoid having 18 year old boys playing against 12 year old boys. The younger boys (being much smaller) would be likely to get crushed in tackles.
2. Have padding around the posts to soften the impact in the event of a collision.
3. Remove obstacles (e.g. broken glass) to avoid cuts.

Identify different measures

If you are asked to identify other measures you can take to reduce risk, be careful to take them from different categories. For example, avoid having two ways of balancing competition, such as boys vs girls or black belt vs green belt in judo.

Worked example

target D

Complete the table below by stating how the competition has been balanced. **(4 marks)**

Competition	How competition has been balanced
Under 19's football tournament	Same age playing against each other
Women's indoor hockey championship	Same sex playing against each other
Judo brown belt competition	Same level competing against each other
Heavyweight boxing competition	Same weight category against each other

'Balanced' in this context is to do with evening out the sides, not remaining steady.

Now try this

target B

It is important that Lucy does not over-exercise as this may lead to injury.

State **four** other different ways that Lucy may avoid injury. **(4 marks)**

Cardiovascular system and exercise

You need to understand the immediate and short-term effects of exercise and physical activity on the cardiovascular system.

The cardiovascular system is:

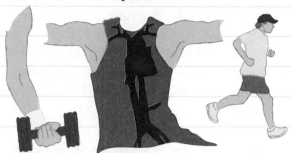

- the heart
- the blood vessels
- the blood.

The cardiovascular system plays an important role during exercise.

Key terms

- HEART RATE = the number of times the heart beats per minute.
- STROKE VOLUME = the amount of blood leaving the heart each beat.
- SYSTOLIC BLOOD PRESSURE = the pressure when blood is being pumped out of the heart.

Note you will not be asked to label a diagram of the heart.

You do not need to differentiate between immediate and short-term effects. They both relate to things that happen to the cardiovascular system STRAIGHT AWAY, i.e. what happens to your heart when you start physical activity.

In response to you starting to exercise, a number of changes to the cardiovascular system happen immediately.
What?

- Increase in heart rate.
- Increase in stroke volume.
- Increase in systolic blood pressure.

Exercise causes an increase in demand on the cardiovascular system. The benefits of these immediate changes are listed below.
Why?

- Increased oxygen delivery and increased removal of carbon dioxide.
- Increased rate of blood flow and therefore increased oxygen delivery.

Worked example

target C

Which of the following is the correct definition of stroke volume? **(1 mark)**

☐ **A** The number of times the heart beats per minute.
☐ **B** The amount of blood pumped around the body during exercise.
☐ **C** The amount of blood pumped out of the heart per minute.
☒ **D** The amount of blood pumped out of the heart per beat.

A = heart rate
B = this is too vague
C = cardiac output

Now try this

target C

Sulliman was aware that when he started to exercise it caused changes to his cardiovascular system.

Give an example of an immediate effect of exercise on Sulliman's cardiovascular system and explain why it alters in this way.

(3 marks)

Cardiovascular system: adaptations 1

You need to understand the long-term effects of regular exercise on the cardiovascular system.

Role of the cardiovascular system

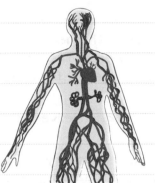

The role of the cardiovascular system during exercise is to:

1. transport oxygen in the blood to the working muscles
2. remove waste products
3. return the blood to the lungs for oxygenation.

Effect of regular exercise

Regular participation in physical activity will result in training adaptations taking place.

'Regular' means more than once a week over a number of weeks. It takes time for adaptations to take place and reversibility will occur if activity reduces or stops.

Adequate REST PERIODS are essential to allow these adaptations to occur.

What are the adaptations?

The adaptations from regular participation in exercise in relation to the cardiovascular system include:

- increase in size and strength of the heart (cardiac hypertrophy)
- increase in stroke volume (amount of blood leaving the heart each beat).

Why are they of benefit?

The benefits of these adaptations are:

- good for health as it reduces the chance of coronary heart disease
- good for fitness as the heart can contract more forcefully
- more blood is ejected from the heart each beat, so there is increased oxygen delivery.

Worked example

target E

Ria plans to sustain her involvement in exercise and physical activity.
Identify one <u>long-term</u> effect of participation in exercise on Ria's heart. **(1 mark)**

Increased strength of the heart

> Make sure you give a long-term effect on the heart

Now try this

target B

Give a potential impact on health of having a stronger heart as a result of regular participation in physical activity. **(1 mark)**

Cardiovascular system: adaptations 2

Other long term training effects on the cardiovascular system caused by regular exercise are outlined below.

Further adaptations relating to the cardiovascular system include:

- lower resting heart rate
- increased MAXIMUM cardiac output during exercise
- faster return to resting heart rate
- increased capillarisation (the development of a capillary network)
- increased number of red blood cells.

The benefits of these adaptations are as follows:

- greater training zone: with an increased stroke volume, the heart needs to beat less often to eject the same amount of blood (see page 50 for more on training zone)
- increased oxygen delivery to working muscles
- more efficient recovery
- increased blood flow supplying oxygen to working muscles.

Cardiac output and stroke volume

To increase cardiac output you can:

Cardiac output is the amount of blood leaving the heart per MINUTE.

increase heart rate

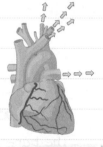

HR = Heart beats per min

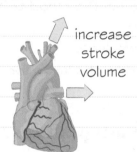

increase stroke volume

SV = Volume per heart beat

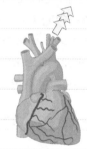

increase both heart rate and stroke volume

---

target B

One of the long-term adaptations of regular participation in physical activity is an increased number of red blood cells.

Explain the benefit of an <u>increase in the number of red blood</u> cells to a <u>long-distance runner</u>.   **(3 marks)**

Long distance running is an endurance activity. This type of running is aerobic, the increased number of red blood cells will help with an increase in transport of oxygen to the working muscles.

Credit is given for recognising the type of activity that requires oxygen.

Now try this

target A

A healthy, active lifestyle will have an impact on the body systems. Describe **four** of the effects of regular participation on the body's cardiovascular system.   **(4 marks)**

Blood pressure and cholesterol

You need to know about the effects of diet on your blood pressure and cholesterol levels, and therefore on your cardiovascular health.

Blood pressure

Blood pressure is the force of the blood pushing against the blood vessel wall as it travels around the body.

SYSTOLIC blood pressure is the pressure in the arteries whilst the heart is contracting.

DIASTOLIC blood pressure is the pressure in the arteries whilst the heart is relaxing and filling with blood.

Diastolic blood pressure is lower than systolic blood pressure because blood flow is slower whilst the heart is relaxing.

If blood pressure is too high it can put a strain on your arteries and heart.

Cholesterol

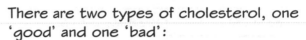

High cholesterol can be caused by having a diet with too much saturated fat. This is found in foods such as butter and fatty meat.

There are two types of cholesterol, one 'good' and one 'bad':

Low density lipoprotein (LDL) is the 'bad' cholesterol that can cause deposits to build up in the arteries. This makes it harder for the blood to circulate and can lead to heart disease.

High density lipoprotein (HDL) is the 'good' cholesterol that can take away cholesterol to be broken down.

Effects of an unhealthy diet

Blood vessels can be negatively affected by an unhealthy diet. Fats can build up in the blood vessels, resulting in high blood pressure and high cholesterol.

A healthy balanced diet will have a positive impact on blood pressure and cholesterol.

Long-term benefits of regular exercise

Regular exercise also benefits blood pressure and cholesterol levels, by:

- lowering resting blood pressure
- lowering cholesterol levels.

These benefits will mean there is a reduced likelihood of a stroke or coronary heart failure.

Worked example

target B

Blood pressure is an important indicator of general health.

Which of the following statements is correct in relation to blood pressure? **(1 mark)**

☐ A An immediate effect of exercise is to decrease blood pressure

☐ B There are three readings of blood pressure: systemic, systolic and diastolic

☒ C Systolic blood pressure will be higher than diastolic blood pressure whilst at rest

☐ D Diastolic blood pressure will be higher than systolic blood pressure whilst at rest

Systolic pressure is the highest because it is when the blood is leaving the heart.

Now try this

target F

If an individual had high levels of LDL ('bad' cholesterol), which of the following should he / she avoid in order to improve his / her health? **(1 mark)**

☐ A Foods high in unsaturated fats (e.g. sunflower oil, nuts)

☐ B Foods high in soluble fibre

☐ C Foods high in saturated fat (e.g. butter, crisps)

☐ D Moderate exercise

Even if you aren't sure, you should be able to work this out by looking at the food examples.

73

Respiratory system and exercise

You need to understand the immediate and short-term effects of exercise and physical activity on the respiratory system.

In response to you starting to exercise, a number of changes to the respiratory system happen immediately.

- Increase in breathing rate (faster breathing).
- Increase in depth of breathing (more air taken in with each breath).

Exercise causes an increase in demand on the respiratory system. The benefits of the immediate changes are:

- increase in removal of carbon dioxide
- increase in the amount of oxygen taken into the lungs in each breath.

Breathed in (%)	Breathed out (%)
Oxygen 21%	Oxygen 16%
Carbon dioxide 0.03%	Carbon dioxide 4%

Explanation of difference in percentages
Less oxygen as used by working muscles
More carbon dioxide is produced as by-product of energy release

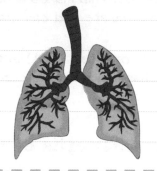

You do not need to learn the tables shown above BUT by knowing them you can explain what happens to oxygen levels during exercise.

Oxygen debt

This is the extra amount of oxygen required AFTER anaerobic exercise, compared with the amount normally needed when at rest.

Remember, oxygen debt does NOT happen during aerobic exercise.

Effect of smoking on the respiratory system

In addition to the risks identified on page 67, smoking will also cause a reduction in oxygen uptake by the red blood cells – they will carry carbon monoxide from the cigarette smoke in preference to oxygen.

Remember it is reduced uptake of oxygen NOT intake – you still breathe in the same amount.

Worked example

target D

Which of the following is <u>not</u> an <u>immediate</u> effect of exercise on the respiratory system?   **(1 mark)**

☐ A Increased breathing rate
☐ B Increased depth of breathing
☒ C Increased lung capacity
☐ D Oxygen debt

Increased lung capacity is a long-term effect of exercise on the respiratory system (see page 75 for more detail).

Now try this

target B

Sulliman was aware that when he started to exercise it caused changes to his respiratory system. Explain the reason for one immediate change in his respiratory system.   **(3 marks)**

Respiratory system: adaptations

You need to understand the long-term training effects of regular exercise on the respiratory system.

There are a number of adaptations to the respiratory system due to regular participation in exercise:

- increased number of alveoli
- increased strength of intercostal muscles
- increased strength of the diaphragm
- increased lung volume (due to increased tidal volume and vital capacity).

The benefits of these adaptations are:

- your respiratory system is stronger
- you can take in more air and extract oxygen more effectively
- therefore you can provide more oxygen for transport to the working muscles.

You do not need to be able to label a diagram of the respiratory system. However, being familiar with it would help you understand the impact of these adaptations.

Lung volumes

Some of the adaptations listed above relate to lung volumes.

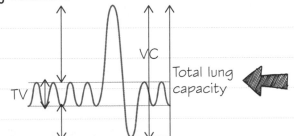

These are the names given to the different parts of the respiratory cycle. You need to know them.

TOTAL LUNG CAPACITY (TLC) = the total volume of air in your lungs after your biggest breath in.

TIDAL VOLUME (TV) = during normal breathing, the total amount breathed in and out in one cycle.

VITAL CAPACITY (VC) = the maximum you can forcibly breathe in and out.

Worked example

target
C

Which of the following is a <u>long-term</u> effect of participation in exercise and physical activity on the respiratory system?   **(1 mark)**

☐ A Increase in blood flow to the lungs
☐ B Increase in oxygen debt
☒ C Increase in vital capacity
☐ D Increase in breathing rate

Option A relates to the cardiovascular system not the respiratory system. Options B and D are immediate effects of exercise.

Now try this

target
B

Outline the impact of an increase in total lung capacity as a result of regular participation in physical activity on an individual.   **(1 mark)**

Antagonistic muscle pairs: biceps and triceps

There are many muscles in the body. You need to know the location and role of some of them.

Antagonistic pairs

Skeletal muscles work together to provide movement of the joints.

While one muscle CONTRACTS, another RELAXES to create movement.

Muscles working together like this are called antagonistic pairs.

The muscle contracting is the AGONIST (prime mover).

The muscle relaxing is the ANTAGONIST.

Remember, muscles are connected to bones via tendons. When the muscles contract, they pull on the tendon which pull on the bone. This creates the movement.

Biceps and triceps

These two muscles are an example of an antagonistic muscle pair.

Name:　　BICEPS

Location:　Front of upper arm.

Role:　　Flexion of the arm at the elbow.

Example:　Upwards phase of a biceps curl.

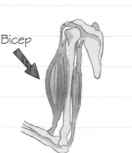 Bicep

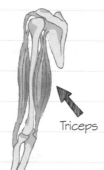 Triceps

Name:　　TRICEPS

Location:　Back of upper arm.

Role:　　Extension of the arm at the elbow.

Example:　Straightening the arms in a chest press.

During this part of the movement, the triceps is the antagonist – it is relaxing to allow the biceps to contract.

During this movement, the biceps is the antagonist – it is relaxing to allow the triceps to contract.

Worked example

target **C**

Explain the term 'antagonistic pair' in relation to muscle movement.　**(1 mark)**

One muscle contracts while the other relaxes to bring about movement.

EXAM ALERT!

Explain the role of EACH muscle in the antagonistic pair.

Students have struggled with exam questions similar to this – **be prepared!**

Results Plus

Now try this

 target **D**

Complete the blanks by identifying the muscles involved in the movement described.　**(2 marks)**

The .... is the agonist when the goalkeeper extends his arm at the elbow and the ....is the antagonist.

Antagonistic muscle pairs: quadriceps and hamstrings

Make sure you know the location and role of these muscles and can give an example of their use.

The quadriceps and hamstring are an antagonistic muscle pair.

Name: QUADRICEPS

Location: Front of upper leg.

Role: Extension of the leg at the knee.

Example: Straightening the leading leg going over a hurdle.

Name: HAMSTRING

Location: Back of upper leg.

Role: Flexion of the leg at the knee.

Example: Bending the trailing leg going over a hurdle.

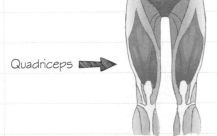

Quadriceps ➡

Hamstring ➡

During this part of the movement the hamstring is the antagonist. It is relaxing to allow the quadriceps to contract.

During this part of the movement the quadriceps is the antagonist. It is relaxing to allow the hamstring to contract.

Different types of joint movement

Skeletal muscles move the body at joints. Words to describe the different types of movement at joints used in this section, e.g. flexion and extension, are explained on pages 84 and 85.

- If you are not sure of the correct spelling of muscle names, write them like they sound.
- Always write the name in full, e.g. quadriceps, not quads.

Worked example

(target E)

Which one of the following muscles is <u>contracting</u> to allow the cyclist in the image to <u>flex</u> his leg at the knee?

(1 mark)

☐ **A** Trapezius
☒ **B** Hamstring
☐ **C** Gastrocnemius
☐ **D** Quadriceps

EXAM ALERT!

Make sure you know the actions of the muscles. Questions often have a picture to help you visualise the movement.

Students have struggled with exam questions similar to this – **be prepared!**   ResultsPlus

Now try this

(target D)

Name the antagonist that is relaxing to allow the cyclist in the image above to flex his leg at the knee.   **(1 mark)**

Gluteals, gastrocnemius and deltoid

Make sure you know the location and role of these muscles and can give an example of their use.

Name: GLUTEAL MUSCLES

Location: Buttocks.

Role: Extension of the leg at the hip.

Example: Lifting the leg back at the hip when running.

Name: GASTROCNEMIUS

Location: Back of lower leg.

Role: Pointing toes (plantar flexion of the ankle) – is basically extension at the ankle.

Example: Pointing toes when performing a straddle jump in trampolining.

Name: DELTOID

Location: The top of the shoulder.

Role: Abducts the arm at the shoulder.

Example: Lifting your arms above your head to block the ball in volleyball.

The diagram below shows the location of these muscles.

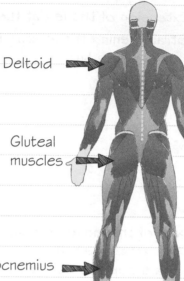

Deltoid

Gluteal muscles

Gastrocnemius

Different types of joint movement

Words to describe the different types of movement at joints, e.g. flexion, extension and abduct, are explained on pages 84 and 85.

Always use the correct name for the gastrocnemius, not the calf. And remember it has a 'C' sound in it Gast...ro**C**....nem...ius

---

Worked example

target **D**

Which **one** of the following muscles is <u>contracting</u> to allow the footballer in the image to <u>extend</u> her leg at <u>the hip</u>?

(1 mark)

☒ **A** Gluteal muscles

☐ **B** Hamstring

☐ **C** Abdominals

☐ **D** Quadriceps

Note that the question refers to the hip, not the knee, and asks about extension rather than flexion.

Now try this

target **C**

Name the movement that occurs when the gastrocnemius contracts and give an example of its use in a game of your choice.

(2 marks)

Trapezius, latissimus dorsi, pectorals and abdominals

Make sure you know the location and role of these muscles and can give an example of their use.

Name: TRAPEZIUS

Location: Upper back, from neck across shoulders.

Role: Rotates the scapula towards the spine.

Example: The butterfly arm action in swimming – when the arms are thrown sideways and backwards out of the water.

Name: LATISSIMUS DORSI

Location: Side of back.

Role: Adducts the upper arm at the shoulder / rotates the humerus.

Example: Bringing arms back to side during a straight jump in trampolining.

Name: PECTORALS

Location: Front of upper chest.

Role: Adducts the arm at the shoulder.

Example: Follow-through from a forehand drive in tennis.

Name: ABDOMINALS

Location: Front of torso, below upper chest.

Role: Flexion of trunk.

Example: Pike dive in diving position.

Worked example

Which one of the following muscles is <u>contracting</u> to allow the tennis player in the image to <u>adduct</u> his arm at the <u>shoulder</u>?   **(1 mark)**

☐ **A** Triceps

☐ **B** Latissimus dorsi

☐ **C** Abdominals

☒ **D** Pectorals

If you are not sure, you can move your own body to help you work out which muscles are the agonists.

Now try this

Name the movement that occurs when the abdominals contract and give an example of its use in a physical activity of your choice.   **(2 marks)**

The muscular system and exercise

You need to know the immediate and short-term effects on the muscular system of participation in exercise and physical activity.

Any physical activity requires movement. All movement is achieved through working the muscles by contracting them. The muscles also need to work to hold the body in a stationary pose.

Muscle contraction

There are two different types of muscle contraction, used for different purposes. You need to know the terms for them and be able to explain the two types.

- ISOTONIC muscle contractions – these are contractions that result in movement.
- ISOMETRIC muscle contractions – these are where the muscles contract but there is no visible movement.

Examples of muscle contractions

- Isotonic contractions, providing movement of the limbs.
- Isometric contractions, where the whole body weight is being held in a balance and there is no movement.

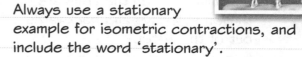

Always use a stationary example for isometric contractions, and include the word 'stationary'.

For example: 'The stationary phase of a rugby scrum is an example of an isometric muscle contraction.'

SHORT-TERM effects of physical activity

- Increase in muscle temperature.
- Increased demand for oxygen (due to additional need for energy).
- Increased production of carbon dioxide (formed as a bi-product during energy release).
- Increased lactic acid production (in anaerobic work).
- Muscle fatigue. Use 'fatigue' rather than 'tire' or 'ache'.

Soft tissue injury

One unwelcome short-term effect of exercise on the muscles could be injury. An injury to the muscle is called a MUSCLE STRAIN. Muscles can also suffer from deep bruising.

Muscle strain can be treated by using techniques such as RICE (see page 89).

MUSCLE ATROPHY can occur if muscles are not used due to injury or inactivity, this is where muscle mass decreases (the opposite to muscle hypertrophy).

(see page 89)

Worked example

 target D

The gymnast in the image is holding a position on the rings. What type of muscle <u>contraction</u> is taking place to allow the gymnast to <u>hold</u> this position? **(2 marks)**

Isometric muscle contraction

EXAM ALERT!

Note that you are looking for muscle 'contraction', not 'action'.

Exam questions similar to this have proved especially tricky in the past – **be prepared!**

Results Plus

Now try this

 target C

Explain a short-term effect of exercise on the muscular system. **(2 marks)**

The muscular system: adaptations

You need to know the effects on the muscular system of regular participation in exercise and physical activity, and its long-term effects.

The adaptations that take place in response to regular exercise include:

* increased strength of muscles
* increased muscle hypertrophy (increased size of muscles)
* increased myoglobin stores.

In addition to the adaptations to the muscular system:

* the tendons and ligaments also become stronger.

The benefits from these adaptations are:

* aids activities requiring strength, power and muscular endurance
* improves immediate oxygen supply to muscles
* better support of joints.

The importance of rest

* It is very important not to overuse muscles, as this can lead to injury (muscle strain).
* ADEQUATE rest is vital for the body to recover between exercise sessions. Only then will the adaptations take place.
* Inadequate rest can have a negative effect on performance.
* Too much rest, whether through injury or general inactivity, can also have a negative effect, causing MUSCLE ATROPHY (wasting).

The importance of protein

Remember that you need to eat protein as part of your balanced diet. Protein is very important to the muscular system as it aids growth and repair of muscles.

If you are asked to discuss the effects of exercise on any of the body systems, make sure you are clear about whether you are referring to short-term / immediate effects, or long-term effects.

target **B**

Which of the following statements identifies the <u>main role</u> of protein in the diet?   **(1 mark)**

☐ **A** Provides the muscles with energy
☒ **B** Helps repair muscles when injured
☐ **C** Prevents muscle fatigue during exercise
☐ **D** Develops atrophy in the muscles as a result of exercise

More than one of these answers are factually correct – so it is really important to choose the MAIN role.

target **B**

Lucy exercises regularly to increase her fitness.

Describe **one** way in which the muscular system is affected by regular exercise and the long-term benefit of this effect on the performer.   **(2 marks)**

Functions of the skeletal system

You should understand the impact of a healthy, active lifestyle on your skeletal system and the role of your skeletal system during physical activity.

Your SKELETAL SYSTEM is made up of the bones of your skeleton.

The FUNCTIONS of the skeleton are to:

- support
- protect
- aid movement.

The skeleton can only be said to AID movement. For movement to occur, you need the skeleton, the ligaments (which connect bone to bone) and the tendons (which connect muscle to bone) to work together.

You need to be able to explain how the skeleton carries out ALL its functions by giving examples of each in relation to physical activity.

Support

Your skeleton provides a frame for your body and therefore supports you. For example, it enables you to balance when performing a handstand.

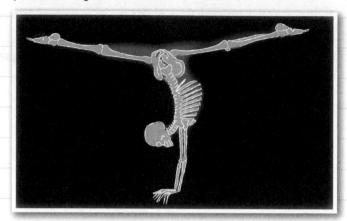

Protection

Your skeleton provides protection for your vital organs, including the heart.

For example, your skull protects your brain if an opponent follows through wildly with their hockey stick and it hits you in the head during a game.

> Always use the words VITAL ORGANS and try to give an example to show your understanding.

Aid movement

1. The bones provide a place for the muscles to ATTACH to, so that when the muscles contract they PULL the bones to cause movement. Movement occurs at the JOINTS of the skeleton.

2. Bones also act as LEVERS. Levers allow the body to increase the force they generate or increase the speed of the movement. This is very helpful in physical activity. For example, a tennis player with longer levers will generate more force on a serve.

Worked example

target G

Which of the following options is correct to complete the sentence below?

The skeletal system protects: **(1 mark)**

- ☐ **A** Vital organs, for example bones, muscles, tendons
- ☒ **B** By providing a hard structure over the organ needing protection
- ☐ **C** By providing a structure for support
- ☐ **D** By producing red blood cells which fight disease

Now try this

target D

The skeletal system has several functions. Explain how the skeleton aids movement.   **(2 marks)**

What you need to know about joints

You need to know the range of movement at HINGE JOINTS, and BALL AND SOCKET JOINTS, during physical activity.

What you need to know about joints

☑ A joint is the place where two or more bones meet. This is where movement can occur.

☑ Although there are many joints in the human body, you only need to know the ones on this page.

☑ You will not be asked to label a skeleton. However, it is useful to know the names of the bones that make up the joints, as that will make it easier for you to describe the joint action or action of muscles.

Joints

You should be able to see the similarities between the two hinge joints and the two ball and socket joints below. The formation of the joint dictates the type of movement that can occur there.

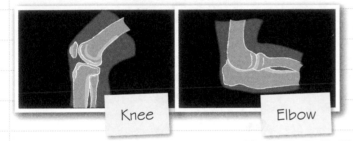

Knee　　　　　　Elbow

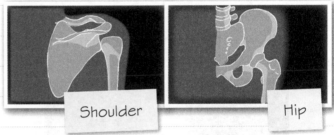

Shoulder　　　　　　Hip

Hinge joints

Located at the:
- knee
- elbow.

Movement at hinge joints:
- flexion
- extension.

Ball and socket joints

Located at the:
- hip
- shoulder.

Movement at ball and socket joints:
- flexion
- rotation
- adduction
- extension
- abduction.

Worked example

target D

Which of the following is <u>not</u> a type of movement associated with hinge joints?　　**(1 mark)**

☐ A　Flexion

☐ B　Extension

☒ C　Abduction

Now try this

target F

What type of joint is formed at the shoulder?　　**(1 mark)**

☐ A　Ball and socket　　　☐ C　Dovetail

☐ B　Ball joint　　　　　　☐ D　Hinge

Range of movement at joints 1

You need to know the RANGE OF MOVEMENT that can be achieved at hinge joints and ball and socket joints.

Joint action: flexion

FLEXION is the term given when the angle at a joint DECREASES.

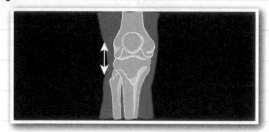

This happens when the bones forming the joint move closer together.

Joint type and application

FLEXION occurs at hinge joints and ball and socket joints.

For example at the knee when the player is preparing to kick a football.

The lower part of your leg gets closer to the upper part of your leg as the angle at the joint decreases.

Joint action: extension

EXTENSION is the term given when the angle at a joint INCREASES.

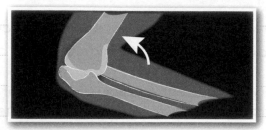

This happens when the bones forming the joint move away from each other.

Joint type and application

EXTENSION occurs at hinge joints and ball and socket joints.

For example at the knee when following through after kicking a football.

The lower part of your leg gets further away from the upper part of your leg as the angle at the joint increases.

Worked example

target E

What is the main <u>range</u> of movement possible at the knee joint? **(1 mark)**

The range of movement at the knee joint is flexion to extension.

Flexion and extension could be written in any order but you do need to include both. If a question asks for the range of movement at a joint, you need to put down both parts because the range is the whole movement covered.

Now try this

target F

Identify the joint action necessary to bend the batting (right) arm at the elbow to move into the position shown in the image. **(1 mark)**

This question asks for the joint action. Watch out for the different terms and make sure you are not confusing joint action with joint type or muscle action.

Range of movement at joints 2

This page covers the other types of movement at ball and socket joints.

Joint actions

ABDUCTION = The movement of a limb AWAY from the midline of the body.

ADDUCTION = the movement of a limb TOWARDS the midline of the body.

ROTATION = when the bone at a joint moves around its own axis, so making a circular movement.

Rotation is really a combination of all of the other joint actions and allows for the biggest range of movement.

Joint type and application

Abduction occurs at ball and socket joints (hip and shoulder).

For example at the shoulder when reaching out sideways to intercept a netball. There is abduction at the shoulder.

To help you remember:
If something is 'abducted', it is taken away.

Adduction occurs at ball and socket joints (hip and shoulder).

For example at the hip in the cross-over leg action when throwing a javelin. The leg comes back towards the midline of the body.

To help you remember:
Adduction starts with 'add', so it is when a limb is added to the midline of the body.

Rotation occurs at ball and socket joints (hip and shoulder).

For example at the shoulder when swimming front crawl. The arm rotates around in a circular motion.

Worked example

target E

Which of the following is the correct term for the <u>joint action</u> that occurs when the ski jumper takes the skis away from the midline of the body to achieve the position shown in the image? **(1 mark)**

☒ **A** Abduction
☐ **B** Adduction
☐ **C** Flexion
☐ **D** Extension

Use the image as a guide – it will have been included to help you.

Now try this

target D

Identify the **three** ranges of movement possible at the shoulder joint. **(1 mark)**

The word 'range' requires the complete movement at the joint.

The skeletal system and exercise

You need to know the benefits weight-bearing exercise and a balanced diet can have on the skeletal system.

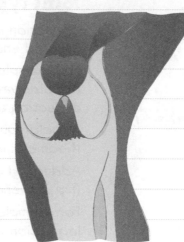

INCREASED BONE DENSITY / STRONGER BONES

STRONGER LIGAMENTS AND TENDONS

- Reduced chance of osteoporosis.
- Better posture.
- Reduced chance of fractures.

- Better support of joints, and therefore more stability during physical activity.
- Regular exercise also increases the production of synovial fluid. This increases lubrication of the joints, aiding flexibility.

Bone density and diet

Bone density is a measurement of the mineral content of the bone – the greater the bone density, the stronger the bone.

Bone density can be improved through a balanced diet containing:

- The mineral CALCIUM – found in many foods including milk and green vegetables (e.g. broccoli).
- VITAMIN D – found in eggs and oily fish. Vitamin D helps the body absorb calcium.

Weight-bearing activities

Weight-bearing activities are those that force your body to work against gravity. They do not include those where your weight is supported, for example cycling.

Weight bearing activities include:

- ☑ walking
- ☑ running
- ☑ tennis
- ☑ aerobics.

Worked example

target D

Which of the following is the **most** beneficial in your diet for ensuring a healthy skeleton?   **(1 mark)**

☒ **A** Vitamin D
☐ **B** Vitamin C
☐ **C** Protein
☐ **D** Carbohydrates

Although all options are important, vitamin D is the most beneficial as it aids an increase in bone density.

Now try this

target B

Using an example, explain why stronger ligaments and tendons will be beneficial to a rugby player.   **(2 marks)**

Potential injuries: fractures

However many measures you take to reduce risk (see pages 68 and 69), injuries can still occur.

Fracture is the correct term for a broken bone.

Fractures happen when the force on the bone is stronger than the bone itself.

There are different types of fracture that can occur, including:

- compound
- greenstick
- simple
- stress.

Symptoms of a fracture may include:

- pain
- bruising
- misshapen limb
- swelling.

When asked to give two different injuries do not say 'break' and 'fracture' – they are the same thing!

simple | compound | stress | greenstick
fracture | fracture | fracture | fracture

Types of fracture

- Compound, or open fractures, are where the broken bone causes the skin to break, adding an additional complication of possible infection.

- Simple, or closed fractures, are where the bone does not break the skin.

- Greenstick fractures are common in younger children. This is where the bone bends on one side and breaks on the other.

- Stress fractures are injuries commonly caused through over-use. This is where a small crack forms in the bone.

Fracture treatment

Bones will mend but they need to be treated by a doctor who will make sure the bone is properly aligned and immobilised usually by a plaster cast until it has healed.

Worked example

target D

Give an example of how a fracture might occur in the following activities. **(2 marks)**

(a) Rugby: Fracture to the leg when landing awkwardly in a tackle.

(b) Cycling: Falling off a bike and putting your arm out to break your fall could cause a fracture of one of the bones of the wrist or arm.

This question is asking for the practical application of fractures to physical activities.

Now try this

target B

Describe **two** named types of fracture. **(4 marks)**

Potential injuries: joint injuries

People who participate in physical activity on a regular basis can also suffer with joint injuries.

Tennis elbow

Tennis elbow is a joint injury where the tendons are inflamed. Pain is felt on the OUTSIDE of the elbow.

Tennis elbow can be caused by poor technique or overuse. For example, repetitive use when playing a backhand in tennis can damage the tendons, resulting in tennis elbow. It can also be caused by activities other than tennis, for example golf or badminton.

Golfer's elbow

Golfer's elbow is another joint injury where the tendons are inflamed. Pain is felt on the INSIDE of the elbow.

Golfer's elbow can be caused by poor technique or overuse, for example excessive practice of a particular shot on a driving range without appropriate rest.

Other activities such as throwing can also result in golfer's elbow.

Dislocation

Dislocations can be very painful. It is where one of the bones at a joint comes out of place.

For example, a dislocated shoulder is when the bone in the upper arm comes away from the shoulder blade

Dislocations are often caused by a fall or blow to the area. For example, falling when running and putting out your arms to save yourself can result in a dislocation at the shoulder.

Symptoms of a dislocation may include:
- pain
- misshapen joint
- swelling.

The importance of rest and recovery

Notice how overuse is often the cause of injuries to the skeletal system. This is why it is so important to include rest as part of your training schedules, so that recovery can take place.

Worked example

target
D

Which is the correct term for a joint injury where the pain is on the <u>outside</u> of the joint?

(1 mark)

☒ A Tennis elbow
☐ B Golfer's elbow
☐ C Tennis knee
☐ D Golfer's knee

Now try this

target
C

Describe a common cause of joint injury and suggest a way to avoid it.

(2 marks)

Potential injuries: sprains and torn cartilage

Other common joint injuries include sprains and torn cartilage. You also need to know about suitable treatments for injuries.

Sprain

A SPRAIN is a joint injury where some of the fibres of the ligament are torn. It happens when the joint goes through a greater range of movement than normal, tearing some of the fibres.

Examples of how sprains can occur:

- forceful twisting
- over-stretching the joint.

SYMPTOMS of a sprain include:

- pain
- bruising
- swelling.

Torn cartilage

TORN CARTILAGE is a joint injury where small tears appear in the cartilage that acts as a cushion at the end of the bones.

Examples of how torn cartilage can occur:

- forceful twisting
- sudden impact / stopping.

Symptoms of torn cartilage include:

- pain
- swelling
- stiffness at the joint.

Treatment

The most appropriate treatment depends on the severity of the injury. More severe injuries will need further medical attention, however a common treatment for joint injuries to reduce the swelling and pain is known as RICE.

- **Rest**
- **Ice**
- **Compression**
- **Elevation.**

Remember to put the components of RICE in the correct order.

Hints and tips

☑ RICE can be used as a temporary measure for dislocations but they must be treated by getting medical help as soon as possible, as damage to surrounding nerves and tissue can happen.

☑ Remember the difference!
  - You can STRAIN a muscle.
  - You can SPRAIN a joint.
    You need to be clear which is which!

☑ Don't forget the importance of calcium and vitamin D in your diet, to help reduce the chance of injury through strong bones, ligaments and tendons.

Worked example

What type of injury is a twisted ankle?   **(1 mark)**

☐ A Fracture
☐ B Deep bruising
☐ C Strain
☒ D Sprain

Now try this

For a named sport, describe how a sprain could occur whilst playing that sport.   **(1 mark)**

EXAM ALERT!

Many students didn't know the difference between a strain and a sprain. Be prepared!

Students have struggled with exam questions similar to this – **be prepared!**   ResultsPlus

Exam skills: multiple choice questions

You will have 1 hour and 30 minutes to complete the full course 5PEO1 exam paper. The paper is worth 80 marks and will contain multiple choice, short answer and extended answer questions. There will be 10 multiple choice questions at the start of the full course paper.

Answering multiple choice questions

☑ Highlight the key words in the question.

☑ Read all the options carefully.

☑ Rule out the ones you know are wrong.

☑ Select what you think is the right answer.

☑ Double check the remaining options as well to make sure you are right.

Choosing the best answers

You need to be really careful when you are choosing your answers. There are often choices which look sensible, but aren't suitable for the CONTEXT of the question. Always read the question carefully and choose the MOST APPROPRIATE options for the context.

Worked example

target F

Nadine plays football. Which of the following fitness tests is <u>most relevant</u> to her sport?

(1 mark)

☐ A Three ball juggle
☐ B Hand grip test
☐ C Standing stork test
☒ D Illinois agility run

This question is asking you to find the most relevant option for the football player.

All of the options test components of health-related exercise or skill-related fitness that are relevant to a footballer. However, options A and B involve the hands and are therefore not the MOST relevant to a footballer.

Option C does involve the legs, but it relates to static balance and therefore is not the MOST relevant option for a footballer.

Option D is the correct answer as it mimics the action used in a game (dodging between players).

This question is asking you to find the <u>most</u> important <u>skill-related</u> component of fitness for the sprinter to get a good start.

First, check all options are skill-related. You can immediately discount options C and D as these are aspects of health-related exercise.

Two options remain. Option B states coordination and, although coordination is required during the race and could impact on the start, it is not as critical for a good start as option A. Without a good reaction time the sprinter will not get a good start.

Always opt for the most obvious correct response.

Worked example

target F

Which of the following is an essential <u>component</u> of <u>skill-related</u> fitness for the sprinter to get a good start? **(1 mark)**

☒ A Reaction time
☐ B Coordination
☐ C Cardiovascular fitness
☐ D Muscular strength

Exam skills: short answer questions

Most questions will require you to write short answers. Some of these may only be one word answers. Others will require short sentences or statements, and occasionally you may be asked to analyse data or to plot a graph. Most short answer questions will be worth 1, 2 or 3 marks each.

Answering short answer questions

☑ Read the question carefully.

☑ Highlight or underline key words.

☑ Note the number of marks available for the question.

☑ Make sure you make the same number of statements as there are marks available. For example, if the question is worth 2 marks, make at least 2 statements.

☑ Don't repeat question words. If you do, make sure you go on to explain in further detail using other words too.

☑ If an activity is referred to in the question, make sure your answers relate to this activity.

☑ Give a range of answers rather than all from the same area (unless asked to do so). For example, if you are asked to give three examples of injury prevention, do not simply state three different safety rules, give a range of answers, for example a specific safety rule, a named item of safety clothing and a specific item of safety equipment.

☑ Use the space available in the answer booklet as a guide. The space provided is plenty – be detailed but concise.

Describe vs explain

Different questions have different command words. If a question asks you to DESCRIBE, it is asking for a simple statement, but if you are asked to EXPLAIN – make sure your answer is developed, and that you give more than a simple statement. You should be using words like BECAUSE or THEREFORE leading you to a more in-depth answer which meets the requirements of explain.

Worked example

target B

Explain why a high level of cardiovascular fitness is beneficial to a long distance runner.

(2 marks)

A high level of cardiovascular fitness is good for long distance runners BECAUSE they will get more oxygen transported to the working muscles, THEREFORE they can use the oxygen to work aerobically and run at a faster pace for longer and improve their performance.

Worked example

target B

One of the possible benefits of a healthy active lifestyle is an increase in self-esteem. Explain how self-esteem can be increased through physical activity.

(2 marks)

Self-esteem is a form of self-confidence. It can be increased through physical activity due to increased levels of serotonin in the brain, THEREFORE as serotonin makes us feel good, you feel better about yourself, increasing your self-esteem.

Note how there are two parts to the answer. The first part explains the term and identifies something that would make you feel better about yourself – serotonin. The second part gives a reason why this would increase self-esteem.

Exam skills: extended answers 1

The full course paper will have two extended answer questions.

Answering extended answer questions

These extended answer questions will NOT have bullet points to guide you in your answer but each question will be phrased so that you can identify the required information for your response if you know the subject area well.

☑ Take time to read the question carefully.

☑ Look for the key words in the question.

☑ Underline / highlight those words that tell you what you need to write about.

☑ Do not just write bullet points.

☑ Do not simply repeat the question words without explaining them.

It is a very good idea to do a quick plan before you write your essay to make sure you cover the key points.

Questions with an *

A question with an * next to it indicates a question that is testing your written communication as well as your knowledge and understanding of the subject.

- You will be assessed on your ability to write a good essay about the topic in the question. You need to use appropriate terminology, for example, if discussing circuit training you should talk about sets and repetitions at stations.

- You need to make sure your essay is well organised, that it flows rather than jumping from one unrelated point to another.

- Spelling, punctuation and grammar should be accurate throughout the essay, but if you make a mistake simply cross it through: you will not be marked down for this.

Your essay does not need to be long. Keep it concise but make sure you make all the necessary points.

Key points to remember

For the extended answer questions, unlike other types of question, you do not get a mark for every point you make.

You are marked on your ability to:

- provide a full and balanced answer (which is why it is so important to identify the key words in a question)

- provide an answer which is well written and shows your full understanding of the topic in the question. Therefore, having identified the key words, it is essential that your response relates to all of them.

Extended answer questions can be based on any area of the specification.

The extended answer questions are designed to stretch you. A series of simple statements will not be enough for full marks.

Key words in the question

There will be an introduction to the question, which outlines the topic area to be looked at. Then there will the actual task. Look for the 'key words' and make sure you are fully covering what they require.

Describe

Describe means that you need to give a description of the major features of the topic area.

Evaluate

Evaluate means you should write about the strengths and weaknesses, or advantages and disadvantages of the topic.

Discuss

Discuss means you should give a number of developed statements, explaining the impact of the topics you have been asked to discuss.

Exam skills: extended answers 2

Here is an example of an extended answer question with a good answer, and some notes to guide you.

Worked example

Miss Saunders is coaching the school netball team and has designed a circuit training programme for the team to follow. Evaluate whether circuit training would be the most appropriate choice of training method for the netball team.   **(6 marks)**

target A

The question requires you to EVALUATE – therefore you need to consider the advantages and disadvantages of using circuit training with a school netball team.

Discussing the benefits of circuit training and why it might be the most appropriate method, is a good way to start

Circuit training could be the most appropriate method because the use of different stations provides a flexible training method. Players can work on fitness and/or skill. They can work at different intensities within the same circuit by altering the number of repetitions. Netball players may need to work on agility to improve their ability to dodge, so 'tailor' a station to reflect this. The whole team can train in the same area, using limited equipment and training principles, such as individual needs and specificity, can be easily applied.

You should end with a conclusion where you make a decision on the most appropriate method and justify your choice.

Then you could go on to discuss other methods of training and why they may be a better choice.

Other methods of training may also be appropriate for netball players, as games players would benefit from fartlek training. This can be adapted to match the changing pace of the game. Cross training could be used to combine circuit training with fartlek training.

Are there any disadvantages to using circuit training?

Circuit training may not be the most appropriate because although skills can be included in the circuit not all players require the same skills, e.g. shooting or defending.

Go for your own personal gold!

Preparing for your PE exam is the same as preparing for any event. So train for it!

Practice

The more you practise (revise), the more you will understand. The more you train, the better your performance.

Pace yourself

You need to peak at the right time, so plan your revision. You can still do other things if you are organised. Put the topics in your diary and stick to the plan.

Don't stay up late the night before your exam: you want to be at your best for your 'event'.

Checklist for exam day

☑ Eat well
☑ Get there early
Remember:
☑ Pens (yes, more than one. They always run out on exam day!)
☑ Pencil – for drawing diagrams or graphs
☑ Ruler
☑ Eraser
☑ Write neatly
☑ Spell as well as you can. If in doubt sound it out and spell the word as it sounds.
Good luck and see you on the podium!

Glossary

Aerobic
'With oxygen'; if exercise is not too fast and is steady, the heart can supply all the oxygen muscles need.

Agility
The ability to change the position of the body quickly and to control the movement of the whole body.

Anabolic steroids
Drugs that mimic the male sex hormone testosterone and promote bone and muscle growth.

Anaerobic
'Without oxygen'; if exercise is done in short, fast bursts, the heart cannot supply blood and oxygen to muscles as fast as the cells use them.

Anorexic
Pertaining to anorexia – a prolonged eating disorder due to loss of appetite.

Balance
The ability to retain the body's centre of mass (gravity) above the base of support with reference to static (stationary), or dynamic (changing), conditions of movement, shape and orientation.

Balanced diet
A diet which contains an optimal ratio of nutrients.

Beta blockers
Drugs that are used to control heart rate and that have a calming and relaxing effect.

Blood pressure
The force exerted by circulating blood on the walls of the blood vessels.

Body composition
The percentage of body weight that is fat, muscle and bone.

Cardiac output
The amount of blood ejected from the heart in one minute.

Cardiovascular fitness
The ability to exercise the entire body for long periods of time.

Competence
The relationship between: skill, the selection and application of skills, tactics, strategies and compositional ideas; and the readiness of the body and mind to cope with the activity. It requires an understanding of how these combine to produce effective performances in different activities and contexts.

Coordination
The ability to use two or more body parts together.

Diuretics
Drugs that elevate the rate of bodily urine excretion.

Ectomorph
A somatotype; individuals with narrow shoulders and narrow hips, characterised by thinness.

Endomorph
A somatotype; individuals with wide hips and narrow shoulders, characterised by fatness.

Erythropoietin (EPO)
A type of peptide hormone that increases the red blood cell count.

Exercise
A form of physical activity done to maintain or improve health and/or physical fi tness, it is not competitive sport.

Fitness
The ability to meet the demands of the environment.

FITT
Frequency, Intensity, Time, Type. (Used to increase the amount of work the body does, in order to achieve overload.)

Flexibility
The range of movement possible at a joint.

Health
A state of complete mental, physical and social wellbeing, and not merely the absence of disease and infirmity.

Healthy, active lifestyle
A lifestyle that contributes positively to physical, mental and social wellbeing, and which includes regular exercise and physical activity.

Heart rate
The number of times the heart beats each minute.

Individual differences / needs
Matching training to the requirements of an individual.

Isometric contractions
Muscle contraction, which results in increased tension but the length does not alter, for example, when pressing against a stationary object.

Isotonic contraction
Muscle contraction that results in limb movement.

Joint
A place where two or more bones meet.

Mesomorph
A somatotype; individuals with wide shoulders and narrow hips, characterised by muscularity.

Methods of training
Interval training, continuous training, circuit training, weight training, fartlek training, cross training.

Muscular endurance
The ability to use voluntary muscles many times without getting tired.

Muscular strength
The amount of force a muscle can exert against a resistance.

Narcotic analgesics
Drugs that can be used to reduce the feeling of pain.

Obese
A term used to describe people who are very overfat.

Overfat
A way of saying you have more body fat than you should have.

Overload
Fitness can only be improved through training more than you normally do.

Overweight
Having weight in excess of normal (not harmful unless accompanied by overfatness).

Oxygen debt
The amount of oxygen consumed during recovery above that which would have ordinarily been consumed in the same time at rest (this results in a shortfall in the oxygen available).

PAR-Q
Physical activity readiness questionnaire.

PEP
Personal Exercise Programme.

Peptide hormones
Drugs that cause the production of other hormones.

Performance
How well a task is completed.

Physical activity
Any form of exercise or movement; physical activity may be planned and structured or unplanned and unstructured (in PE we are concerned with planned and structured physical activity, such as a fitness class).

Power
The ability to do strength performances quickly (power = strength × speed).

Progressive overload
To gradually increase the amount of overload so that fitness gains occur, but without potential for injury.

Protocol
The procedure for carrying out a test.

Reaction time
The time between the presentation of a stimulus and the onset of a movement.

Reversibility
Any adaptation that takes place as a consequence of training will be reversed when you stop training.

Recovery
The time required for the repair of damage to the body caused by training or competition.

Rest
The period of time allotted to recovery.

RICE
Rest, Ice, Compression, Elevation (a method of treating injuries).

Self-esteem
Respect for, or a favourable opinion of, oneself.

SMART
Specific, Measurable, Achievable, Realistic, Time-bound.

Somatotypes
Classification of body type.

Specificity
Matching training to the requirements of an activity.

Speed
The differential rate at which an individual is able to perform a movement or cover a distance in a period of time.

Stimulants
Drugs that have an effect on the central nervous system, such as increased mental and/or physical alertness.

Stroke volume
The volume of blood pumped out of the heart by each ventricle during one contraction.

Target zone
The range within which an individual needs to work for aerobic training to take place (60–80 per cent of maximum heart rate).

Training
A well-planned programme which uses scientific principles to improve performance, skill, game ability and motor and physical fitness.

Training thresholds
The boundaries of the target zone.

Underweight
Weighing less than is normal, healthy or required.

Answers

The following pages contain examples of answers that could be made to the *Now try this* questions throughout the revision guide. In many cases these are not the only correct answers.

1. Health and physical activity

Type of benefit	Benefit for someone at school	Benefit for someone at work
Social	Learn how to mix and get on with others	Opportunity to increase social network
Mental	Increase self confidence because improving	Relieve stress from pressure of work
Physical	Improve cardiovascular fitness	Reduce resting blood pressure

2. Mental benefits of an active lifestyle

Self-esteem means how much confidence you have about yourself. When you exercise more you will start to become fitter, this can make you feel better about yourself increasing your self-esteem.

3. Mental and physical benefits

When you find something really difficult to do this presents a challenge. For example, if you were afraid of heights, rock climbing would present a physical challenge because you would need to overcome your mental fear and have the physical exertion of taking part in the activity.

4. Fitness benefits of an active lifestyle

C and F.

5. Health benefits of an active lifestyle

Less chance of suffering from coronary heart disease.
Less chance of suffering from osteoporosis.
Less chance of suffering a stroke.

6. Social benefits of an active lifestyle

A social benefit is increased cooperation. If you can work with others without arguing, this will increase enjoyment. Another social benefit is making new friends, if you have friends rather than going to a club on your own you can interact more with others and have fun.

7. Key influences: people

Brooklyn is influenced by his family. Brooklyn's dad is a professional footballer who trains and plays as his work so Brooklyn would have been introduced to football when he was young and continued playing it.

8. Key influences: image

C

9. Key influences: culture

In some cultures women are not encouraged to participate in sport therefore fewer girls from these cultures are likely to choose to participate. Some sports are not as popular as others in some cultures. For example, table tennis is very popular in some Asian countries, therefore it is more likely you will play the popular sport within your culture. Although lots of people with disabilities do participate in physical activity their choice may be more limited due to availability of clubs running sessions for adapted sports, thus they are more likely to choose activities more easily available.

10. Key influences: resources

C

11. Key influences: health and wellbeing and socio-economic

If the family has a high socio-economic status they will be able to afford more expensive sports such as horse-riding, tennis and skiing. If the family has a low socio-economic status they are less likely to choose these activities.

12. Roles and required qualities

The range of roles includes performing, volunteering, leading and officiating. Most people like to play so take that role but if you don't like to play you can coach or referee a match. Also if you get injured you can change role from performer to coach therefore remaining in physical activity.

13. Sports participation pyramid 1

(a) Stage 3 = Participation.

(b) Stage 4 = Foundation.

14. Sports participation pyramid 2

Only a limited number of people will have the skills to achieve this level. Not all those that have the skills will have the right level of determination and therefore will not train enough.

15. Initiatives and their common purposes

Retain people in sport therefore not losing people as they get older or injured, giving them opportunity through club network to stay involved.

16. Agencies

Increase participation, retain people in sport, create opportunities for talented performers to achieve success.

17. Health, fitness and exercise

D

18. Health, fitness and exercise and a balanced healthy lifestyle

Provided you exercise sensibly, in other words have appropriate rest times between sessions, regular exercise can bring a number of health benefits. These benefits could be physical, social or mental. For example, weight bearing exercise can reduce the chance of having osteoporosis later in life.

19. Cardiovascular fitness and muscular endurance

C

20. Muscular strength, flexibility and body composition

Muscular strength is the missing component of health-related exercise.

21. Agility, balance and coordination

Balance is the ability to retain the body's centre of gravity above the base of support. This is important when moving and changing direction quickly, otherwise a performer would fall over rather than be able to control the movement.

22. Power, reaction time and speed 1

The ability to do strength performances quickly (power = strength × speed). High jump to get explosive lift from the floor to gain more height.

23. Effects of cardiovascular fitness and muscle endurance

Cardiovascular fitness is the ability to exercise the entire body for long periods of time without tiring. Muscle endurance is the ability to use voluntary muscles many times without getting tired.

Cardiovascular fitness is used in order for Ashley to complete the 3 km every session. Muscular endurance is used in his legs to allow him to keep working his leg muscles to complete the 3 km.

24. Effects of muscular strength, flexibility and body composition

A

25. Effects of agility, balance and coordination

Hand (holding club) and eye to allow them to get the ball in the hole.

Arms and legs to ensure efficient stroke.

Feet and arms to ensure efficient movement allowing greater generation of power.

26. Power, reaction time and speed 2

100 m sprinter	Needs to start the race as soon as possible after the gun, even a slight delay at the start could lose the race.
Midfielder	Good reaction time could be an advantage, but the game will not be lost if one player has a poor reaction time.
Gymnast	Gymnasts will only need reaction time if an error has been made.

27. PAR-Q and fitness tests

Need to know this because if there has been a history of illness, the individual may have a heart condition without knowing. This could put them at risk if exercise is too intense.

28. Fitness tests 1

(a) Harvard Step Test

(b) Cooper's 12-minute run test

(c) Treadmill test

29. Fitness tests 2

First it would be used to identify his rating, which is below average. Then his rating would be used to decide if this was an area of health-related exercise he needed to work on.

30. Fitness tests 3

Illinois Agility Run test mimics dodging movement in a game when swerving in and out of cones therefore measures skill required in game, making it a valid test for a footballer.

31. Fitness tests 4

The standing board jump measures power. You have to stand behind a line and take off using a two-footed take-off. You mark where you land and then measure from the start line to where you landed.

32. Fitness tests 5

The ruler drop test is a test for reaction time.

The person taking the test would stand with their hand ready to catch the ruler, the 0 cm mark between their thumb and forefinger. When the ruler is dropped they catch it as soon as possible and the distance from 0 cm is measured and compared to a chart to show the rating.

33. Principles of training: progressive overload

Jamie should measure how much he works his cardiovascular fitness during a session and then increase this amount slightly on the next session. He should continue to gradually increase how hard he works when he finds that he can manage the workload relatively easily and his cardiovascular fitness should continue to gradually improve.

Answers

34. Principles of training: specificity

Exercise bike is most likely to be used, as it most closely matches the required actions of the sport so when cycling on the bike the cyclist is training the same muscles they will use in their event.

35. Principles of training: individual differences / rest and recovery

Extended writing question: Need to be well written, balanced, in sentences (not bullet points) and have a conclusion. The content could include:

- rest – period of time allocated to recovery; recovery – time required for repair of damage to the body
- important because it is needed to plan adequate rest to allow recovery
- e.g. build in rest days by training alternate days which would allow an individual to replenish energy stores
- appropriate levels of rest also allows adaptations to take place as a result of training
- example adaptations could be increased strength if following a weight training programme
- adequate rest also reduces feelings of fatigue and allows the performer to de-stress so they are more motivated to train
- adequate rest also prevents overtraining therefore reduces chance of injury so that training is not interrupted.

36. Principles of training: FITT principle and reversibility

D

37. Value of goal setting and SMART targets

So you can see if you have achieved your target.

38. SMART targets

Realistic

39. Interval training

Breaks are built into the session.

The breaks allow recovery.

The session is made up of sets of reps of work periods and rest periods.

40. Continuous training

Continuous training develops cardiovascular fitness and muscular endurance, both of which are required in long distance running.

41. Fartlek training

Include sprinting to mirror what you need to do in a game, for example, sprint 20 m to mimic losing a marker and sprinting for a free ball in a game.

Include jogging to mirror recovery parts in a game after a period of high intensity like when you jog back into position.

42. Circuit training

Organise different exercises at stations. Work on each station for a set period of time before moving on to the next station. Can be fitness-based on skill-based.

43. Weight training

To increase muscular strength you need fewer repetitions but greater resistance or heavier weights. To increase muscular endurance rather than muscular strength you would increase the number of repetitions and reduce the weight lifted so your muscles got used to working for longer periods of time.

44. Cross training

B

45. Exercise session: warm-up

B

46. Exercise session: main session and cool-down

after, two, jogging, stretching, soreness, flexibility

47. Exercise session: endurance

No rest so running is continuous and never over 60% maximum, therefore must be for endurance.

48. Exercise session: power

Running is at 85% of maximum pace and requires a walk for recovery, therefore must be for power event involving sprinting.

49. Heart rates and graphs

(a) Student C

(b) Student A

(c) Student C

50. Setting training target zones

Lines B and C.

51. Requirements of a balanced diet

If you don't eat a balanced diet you could develop a mineral deficiency such as anaemia.

52. Macronutrients

1 You need to make sure you eat enough carbohydrates to give you the energy you need to exercise.

2 The macronutrients are carbohydrates, fats and proteins. Fats and carbohydrates are used to provide energy, therefore allow us to be active; protein is used for muscle growth and tissue repair so helps us to remain healthy.

53. Micronutrients

B

54. Timing of dietary intake

Blood is moved from the digestive system to the active muscles, so the performer will not be able to digest their food properly.

55. Redistribution of blood flow

Blood shunting, increased blood flow.

56. Mesomorphs

1 Increased muscle mass for more power so that the tennis player can make the ball travel faster, making it harder to return.

2 Rugby.

57. Ectomorphs and endomorphs

1 Events where additional weight makes it harder for your opposition e.g. some positions in rugby, or sumo wrestling.

2 They would be slower than someone with an ectomorph body type so their performance would deteriorate. This is because they would be carrying excess body weight therefore slowing them down.

58. Factors affecting optimum weight

Dense bones are heavy, some people have larger bones than others therefore they will weigh more; their optimum weight will be heavier than someone with smaller bones.

59. Anorexia and underweight

They will follow a balanced diet eating the right amount and type of foods.

They will have good self-esteem as a result of their lifestyle and not be obsessive about their body image.

60. Overweight, overfat, obese

1 Heart disease, type 2 diabetes.

2 By having more body fat than you should you are making your body work harder, therefore energy supply will deplete sooner making it difficult to participate in physical activity. This will mean fitness cannot increase so the individual is less likely to be motivated to sustain involvement.

61. Anabolic steroids

Liver damage, testicular atrophy.

62. Beta blockers

They have a calming effect allowing heart rate to slow down.

63. Diuretics

C

64. Narcotic analgesics

Narcotic analgesics.

65. Stimulants

If they have had a long season and are tired but need to be alert for a big event they may take stimulants.

66. Peptide hormones

It increases their red blood cell count which means the runner will be able to carry more oxygen so they can maintain a good energy supply throughout the race,

allowing them to maintain a better pace and run the distance more quickly.

67. Recreational drugs

Bronchitis, emphysema.

68. Reducing risk through personal readiness

Fractured shin: wear shin pads to reduce impact of kick to leg

Soft tissue injury: warm up to increase elasticity of muscle.

69. Reducing risk through other measures

Correct clothing; warm up; correct equipment; correct facilities.

70. Cardiovascular system and exercise

There would be an increased heart rate so that blood flowed around the body faster, allowing for an increase in oxygen delivery to the working muscles and quicker removal of carbon dioxide.

71. Cardiovascular system: adaptations 1

Good for health, for example there is a reduced chance of suffering with coronary heart disease.

72. Cardiovascular system: adaptations 2

Lower resting heart rate; faster return to resting heart rate; increased capillarisation; increased number of red blood cells.

73. Blood pressure and cholesterol

C

74. Respiratory system and exercise

When you exercise you need more oxygen than when you are resting. Therefore his breathing rate would increase, so that more air containing oxygen could enter the lungs so more oxygen could be transported to the working muscles.

75. Respiratory system: adaptations

Take in more air, allowing them to extract more oxygen for transport to the working muscles.

76. Antagonistic muscle pairs: biceps and triceps

Triceps is agonist, biceps is antagonist.

77. Antagonistic muscle pairs: quadriceps and hamstrings

Quadriceps

78. Gluteals, gastrocnemius and deltoid

Pointing the toes, kicking a football with the laces.

79. Trapezius, latissimus dorsi, pectorals and abdominals

The flexion of trunk, upward phase of a sit-up.

80. The muscular system and exercise

Increased demand for oxygen due to additional need for energy during exercise.

81. The muscular system: adaptations

Effect: increased size in muscle,
Benefit: increased strength.

82. Functions of the skeletal system

The skeleton is made up of joints and movement occurs at these joints. The skeleton also provides a place for muscle attachment allowing movement.

83. What you need to know about joints

A

84. Range of movement at joints 1

Flexion

85. Range of movement at joints 2

Flexion to extension, abduction to adduction, rotation.

86. The skeletal system and exercise

Increased stability of the joint; less likely to gain an injury when being tackled.

87. Potential injuries: fractures

Greenstick fractures – the bone bends on one side and breaks on the other.

Stress fractures – a small crack forms in the bone.

88. Potential injuries: joint injuries

Overuse – allow rest and recovery.

89. Potential injuries: sprains and torn cartilage

Hockey – accidently stepping on the ball and your ankle going over causing it to twist at the joint.

Your own notes

Published by Pearson Education Limited, Edinburgh Gate, Harlow, Essex, CM20 2JE.

www.pearsonschoolsandfecolleges.co.uk

Copies of official specifications for all Edexcel qualifications may be found on the Edexcel website: www.edexcel.com

Text and original illustrations © Pearson Education Limited 2012
Edited and produced by Wearset, Boldon, Tyne and Wear
Illustrated and typeset by HL Studios, Witney, Oxfordshire
Cover illustration by Miriam Sturdee

The right of Jan Simister to be identified as author of this work has been asserted by her in accordance with the Copyright, Designs and Patents Act 1988.

First published 2012

16 15
10

British Library Cataloguing in Publication Data
A catalogue record for this book is available from the British Library

ISBN 978 1 446 90362 9

Printed in Slovakia by Neografia

Acknowledgements
The author and publisher would like to thank the following individuals and organisations for permission to reproduce photographs:

(Key: b-bottom; c-centre; l-left; r-right; t-top)

Alamy Images: Allstar Picture Library 7br, Ingram Publishing 25, Richard G. Bingham II 27, Stock Image. Pixland 62; Corbis: Patrik Giardino 61l; **Getty Images:** 79, Anderson Ross 62l, Bellurget Jean Louis 30, Davis Madison 76, George Doyle 34br, Getty Images Sport / Al Bello 21l, Mike Harrington 63l, Mike Powell 56, 66t, technotr 85; **Masterfile UK Ltd:** 80tr; **Shutterstock.com:** Aleksandar Todorovic 61r, CHEN WS 24r, CLS Design 78, Diego Cervo 34bc, Jiang Dao Hua 21c, Lisa F. Young 10, Maxisport 24l, Michael Klenetsky 84, Mikhail Pogosov 63r, Orange Line Media 34bl, Peter Bernik 90, Photo works 7bl, Sportgraphic 57, Supri Suharjoto 21r, Suzanne Tucker 66b, tankist276 80cr, 80br, tankist276 80cr, 80br; **Sport England:** 16l; **www.imagesource.com:** 12, Corbis RF Value 77; **Youth Sport Trust:** 16r

All other images © Pearson Education

Every effort has been made to contact copyright holders of material reproduced in this book. Any omissions will be rectified in subsequent printings if notice is given to the publishers.

In the writing of this book, no Edexcel examiners authored sections relevant to examination papers for which they have responsibility.